BUSINESS LITIGATION DEMYSTIFIED

Diane Cafferata

Little Phoenix Publishing, 2020

Editor: Katie Chambers of Beacon Point Services

Production Team: Danielle Decker of Decker's Word Shop
and Jen Henderson of Wild Words Formatting

Cover Design: Ryan Lause

ISBN:

978-1-7349761-0-6 (e-book)
978-1-7349761-1-3 (print)

BUSINESS LITIGATION DEMYSTIFIED

As a thank you for downloading my book,
I would like to give you my Checklist
"Getting the Best Out of Outside Litigation Counsel" for free.

Visit litdemystified.com/checklists to Download

For those who are truly courageous in the face of adversity.

DISCLAIMER

This book is presented solely for educational purposes. Neither the author nor the publisher is offering it as legal or other professional services advice. While the author has put forth her best efforts in preparing this book, the author and publisher make no representations or warranties of any kind and assume no liabilities of any kind with respect to the accuracy and completeness of the contents and specifically disclaim any implied warranties of merchantability or fitness of use for a particular purpose. Neither the author nor the publisher shall be held liable or responsible to any person or entity with respect to any loss or incidental or consequential damages caused, or alleged to have been caused, directly or indirectly, by the information contained herein. No warranty may be created or extended by sales representatives or written sales materials. Every company is different and the advice and strategies contained herein may not be suitable for your situation. You should seek the services of a competent professional—ideally a trial lawyer—and this book will merely help you work with them.

Although I am a lawyer, I'm not your lawyer. Nothing in this book creates an attorney-client relationship between us. This book should not be used as a substitute for the advice of a competent litigation attorney admitted or authorized to practice in your jurisdiction.

Further, this book and the views and opinions in it are not endorsed, blessed or even necessarily shared by members of Quinn Emanuel Urquhart & Sullivan LLP. No statement or omission in this book should be attributed to anyone else but me—and even then, remember the whole point of this book is to provide generalized background information and not any particular advice.

TABLE OF CONTENTS

CHAPTER ONE

WHY THIS BOOK?

This book was designed for anyone who would like to quickly sharpen their understanding of the litigation process, as well as learn some of the key dynamics around developing a winning litigation strategy, without investing a great deal of time in doing so.

The main audience for this book is:

- U.S. and foreign company executives, officers, and employees

- U.S. and foreign in-house counsel

It will also be beneficial for:

- law students or young litigators

- outside lawyers unfamiliar with litigation

- litigation experts and consultants

- litigation vendors

- anyone who wants to be better informed and empowered in the event of litigation

This book is absolutely going to give you a solid foundational understanding of the U.S. litigation process in a quick and easy read. One executive who read it texted me, "I think I am ready for litigation. Bring it on!"

I promise you this book will enable you to:

- Make better decisions and recommendations about the selection of litigation counsel

- Steer the company away from litigation by dealing with threats effectively before being sued

- Ask better questions of the company's litigation counsel

- Recognize opportunities afforded by undeveloped facts

- Provide better advice to employees collecting materials, preparing for deposition, assisting with strategy

- Better understand the contents of legal bills

- Explain to others at the company the significance of events in the litigation

- Explain to others at the company what is being spent on the litigation and why

- Mitigate risk for the company by creating policies based on a better understanding of possible litigation threats

- Better manage stress

Why Learn More About the Litigation Process?

Litigation refers to the process of resolving disputes. It broadly encompasses resolution activities from pre-suit investigation through appeal or settlement and counseling. Litigation is thus distinguishable from regulatory, compliance, and transactional work also performed by lawyers.

Litigation creates risk, uncertainty, substantial cost, and business distraction

Running a business successfully, large or small, depends to some degree on legal advice. Even fairly small- to mid-sized businesses find themselves dealing with legal issues, such as compliance activities, employment counseling, contract interpretation, deal negotiation, and litigation.

Each of these subjects may be challenging and present risks for the company, as litigation often represents a relatively high level of risk and significant cost, distraction, and stress for a company's management and employees. Litigation over a company's practices can threaten or eclipse its business, or even destroy it.

Moreover, litigation is heavily dependent on procedural rules and the activities of a motivated adversary. Its outcome is primarily contingent on a myriad of decisions by an authoritative and extremely busy judge and ultimately may hinge on the decision of the jury.

And since most companies will find themselves in litigation sooner or later—this is true even if they are proactive in managing their employees, customers, and other business relationships—it is wise for them to have general familiarity with the litigation process.

Corporate disputes can arise from many sources: employees, former employees, independent contractors, customers, consumers, shareholders, competitors, business partners, and the government.

Typical subjects of large corporate disputes include: patents, trademarks, trade secrets and other intellectual property rights, contractual obligations and rights, financial and regulatory disclosures and compliance, gender and other types of discrimination, products liability and other tort claims, environmental issues, and unfair competition, to name a few.

Executives, Employees, and Even In-House Counsel May Have Little Experience with Litigation

> **In-house counsel** refers to lawyers who are employees of a company and handle or manage that company's legal issues.
>
> Sometimes in-house counsel directs litigation from inside the company, but often in-house counsel hires a law firm to bring or defend itself in litigation with third parties.
>
> The lawyers hired for that purpose are referred to as **outside counsel**, or simply **litigation counsel**.

Yet as pervasive and challenging as litigation can be, for many executives and employees, litigation is more or less a black box.

In a smaller company without its own in-house counsel, it may hire a litigation team and rely completely on that team for its understanding of options in the litigation. It may defer heavily to outside counsel simply because it does not feel equipped to do otherwise.

In larger companies, the company will rely on the expertise of its in-house counsel to supervise the outside litigation team. The in-house counsel will likely rely heavily on outside counsel as well, for the simple reasons that they are terribly busy, have many other legal issues to deal with, and the outside team is in a better position to manage the day-to-day of the litigation.

This state of affairs is okay. It happens all the time and we survive it.

But it's like a patient and doctor. The doctor can just provide advice to the patient, but if the patient were more informed about the basics, then the patient can better understand and participate in the process.

Company executives may be saying, "I don't need to know this. This is why we have in-house counsel." But by achieving a basic understanding of the process, these executives can have richer discussions with their in-house counsel. They will have a more sophisticated view of the company's options throughout the case and some of the decisions being made around the litigation.

This book will help certain in-house counsel as well, such as those with limited or only very general experience actually practicing or supervising civil litigation.

In-house counsel might seek to have greater familiarity with the litigation process for many reasons, not the least of which is that their expertise lies primarily in other areas. For example, a social media company may have an ongoing need for in-house counsel with substantial intellectual property and privacy law expertise. A company with frequent corporate and real estate acquisitions may need an in-house team with ample transactional and real estate experience. Although the in-house team in such situations might have *some* prior litigation experience, it's often not efficient for such companies to employ full-time litigation experts in-house.

By way of further example, many companies are well served by hiring more junior in-house lawyers and "raising" them within the company so they become experts in the company's business and operations. However, an attorney who has joined a company after just a few years of experience in an outside law firm will not have the same litigation expertise as more seasoned outside counsel.

Finally, even in-house lawyers with litigation experience often have experience only up until the point of settlement, but less frequently up through trial. Understanding the process through trial or arbitration is critical to handling or supervising the many preceding steps well. And proper management of the pretrial phase can lead to faster and more advantageous settlements.

Lack of Familiarity with Litigation Has Many Negative Consequences

Crazy Stress

I asked my friend Janie, who had been in-house counsel for a tech company, what she remembered keeping her up at night while serving in that role. Without hesitation, she answered, "Uh, going to jail!"

> **General counsel** usually refers to the highest level of in-house counsel within a company. It can also refer to an outside lawyer who serves in that role for a company.

Executives and general counsel in public companies are required to certify the financials for the company. Sadly, they may not understand them completely and must rely in significant part on the general capabilities and integrity of their colleagues in the finance department.

Supervising a bet-the-company case or other litigation of strategic significance to the company requires a similar level of nervous trust with respect to many decisions. In such situations, decision-making is even more intense because the company is in crisis mode. This is not an optimal way to make decisions.

The fact that outside counsel is often hired to handle corporate litigation does not take the pressure off in-house counsel either. It adds to the pressure by making in-house counsel "responsible" for the activities of many lawyers without having direct supervision of them.

Inability to Participate Meaningfully or Fully

Also, company personnel will be less effective in developing facts, or arguments based on those facts, than they would be if they were familiar with the general procedural framework of the process.

This can deprive a company of its best arguments because the creativity of those inside the company—those in the best position to have or to gather the salient facts—is not fully engaged.

Outside counsel functions better when they are deeply familiar with their client's business because it helps them formulate more successful legal strategies and make better-informed legal decisions on behalf of the client. Similarly, a client who understands the basics of the litigation process will be more effective in assisting counsel to develop the facts.

Poor Selection of Litigation Counsel

Next, young companies new to litigation frequently turn to the same firm they used as their "deal counsel." They ask those that helped them incorporate, created simple employment agreements, or negotiated their joint venture, etc., to refer them to a litigator. Thus, they wind up with a litigator at that same firm.

But even if those transactional lawyers were terrific, that does not mean the firm's litigators are well placed to handle the suit. Nor does it mean they can deal effectively with larger strategic considerations that may be implicated.

With little understanding of the litigation process, executives and in-house counsel may be at a loss when selecting litigation counsel, so they go for the lowest price because they are not sure what other factors to consider. This is not a good way to select counsel.

Poor Control of Litigation Costs

Litigation is very costly. In-house counsel, or whoever is supervising the outside litigation team, will be expected to control litigation costs. This is difficult for anyone because the cost of litigation is largely driven by adversaries and the judge.

Without an understanding of litigation, it is difficult for those supervisors to discuss with outside counsel the many options available and effectively weigh into decisions.

Further, in-house counsel may struggle to justify their decisions and the cost to the C-Suite. Or in-house counsel may feel pressured by the

C-Suite *not* to settle a matter over a certain dollar amount, which in the long run could be a very expensive mistake if that threshold is not realistic given the costs and risks of proceeding with a dispute.

Missed Negotiation / Avoidance Opportunities

Pre-litigation communications and discussions with a potential adversary can, if not handled appropriately, cause litigation to break out. If a business misses opportunities to shortcut the dispute before it starts, it may find itself in litigation that could have been avoided.

Poor Risk Avoidance

Litigation represents a huge proportion of the overall legal risk a company faces. Without a greater understanding of the litigation process, its executives and even in-house counsel may not recognize, or take advantage of, opportunities to avoid a dispute altogether.

Difficulty Counseling Employees

Without a thorough understanding of the context of the litigation and why various litigation events are important, in-house counsel and executives may have trouble alleviating employees' frustration about the time and stress involved with pursuing or defending the litigation. This means more lost opportunities and more business disruption.

These are just a few potential consequences. Obviously, any time you are moving through a stressful, risky, expensive situation that threatens the viability of your business, it would be better to understand the basics and be an engaged participant rather than feeling like the litigation is sweeping you along.

How the Reader Will Benefit From This Book

This book is a detailed overview, just right for quickly creating a level of understanding that remedies these problems.

To make a simple analogy with Google maps, this book presents litigation procedure at the approximate level of countries and U.S. states. No counties or cities in this book!

Now, most law books only cover one state or one county, and then the entire book deals with intricate cities and streets. This level of specificity is not accessible to most company personnel. Even in-house counsel may not have the time or inclination to make such a deep dive.

This book deliberately stays at a higher level. It is intended to give anyone a solid and understandable overview of how the process works and what the basic litigation tools are and how they work.

Armed with this understanding:

- Executives or in-house counsel will be able to start taking proactive steps the minute a dispute begins to brew. If they are generally familiar with litigation, they can be thinking actively with their outside litigation counsel about creative ways to head off the conflict.

- They will not have to be dependent on outside counsel for an understanding of where the process is leading at any given time. Instead, an executive that has read this book will understand the process, what stage the company is in, and how each stage relates to the next.

- Being meaningfully engaged from the start, the executive or in-house counsel will be in a better position to select litigation counsel and have better, more sophisticated questions for their litigators. They will recognize helpful evidence and bring it to the litigators' attention because they will be thinking more productively about the litigation.

- They will also be better able to articulate to others at the company the significance of litigation activities coming up. They will counsel employees more effectively because they are in a better position to explain the significance of events in the litigation, easing stress and disruption.

- In turn, this means others at the organization will become more creative in thinking about litigation-related problems and aware of opportunities they would have otherwise missed. They too will be in a better position to ask meaningful questions of outside litigation counsel or of those supervising the litigation effort. They will also know when to inform litigation counsel of facts that might be pertinent or decisions that could impact the ongoing litigation.

- The reader will better understand the litigation invoices and how to make decisions along the way that focus litigation efforts. This will give their company more bang for its litigation buck, instead of receiving sky-high legal bills and wondering how so much money was spent.

- Having some familiarity with litigation, they will be tuned to recognize possible litigation issues and create policies and procedures that head off those risks.

Trust Me!

In twenty years at the world's foremost litigation shop, I have run and tried numerous litigation cases across a broad range of subjects. I have represented large companies including Samsung, Lehman Brothers, Qualcomm, and Mattel, as well as companies with just a handful of employees. I have counseled in-house personnel, company executives, and individual litigants in litigation matters.

I have also had the privilege of litigating cases across the country, including New York, Los Angeles, Boston, San Diego, San Francisco, Illinois, Texas, Arizona, Delaware, Washington, D.C., and the Marshall Islands. These have included more than my fair share of bet-the-company cases, global strategic litigation, and other highly complex disputes. Several of my cases have involved trials that took several weeks to try. Some of my cases have involved the application of foreign law, including the law of Israel, Hungary, Taiwan, Australia, Saudi Arabia, India, Hong Kong, Singapore and Japan.

This broad and lengthy experience puts me in a good position to speak to civil procedure in general and identify the commonalities between U.S. jurisdictions. Certain litigation patterns play out over time too, which I've shared in this book, along with some good ways to deal with them. Throughout my practice, I've focused on finding creative solutions for clients that help to control their litigation costs.

Over and over again, I have seen that a better understanding of litigation enhances litigation results. If the in-house counsel I'm working with has a litigation background, I will likely have a different quality of conversation with them than I would with a former transactional lawyer.

When talking with the in-house attorney with previous litigation experience, there is a base level of understanding about what is going on in the dispute and how it fits into the big picture, which can become a launchpad for a more active conversation, say, about concerns with particular witnesses or where factual evidence on a certain point might be found. Every substantive conversation with them about the case is enhanced, and this translates to better coordination and better results.

Also, the challenging litigation questions that come up in my cases routinely call for out-of-the-box thinking on the part of not only outside litigation counsel but also by in-house counsel and company personnel as well. Bringing these groups more into synch with each other inevitably means better communication, better ideas, and better results.

This Book <u>Will</u> Improve Your Litigation Management Skills

This book primarily deals with civil cases at the trial court level. This is where discovery takes place, where motion practice shapes the case, and where evidence is ultimately taken through the presentation of live witnesses and admission of documents. Focusing on this level means covering all of these basic litigation activities.

> **Civil matters** deal with wrongs by a private party, like a breach of contract or negligence, and offer remedies such as compensation, punitive damages, and injunctive relief. Civil matters are distinguishable from criminal matters, where the defendant is accused of illegal conduct and risks fine and/or imprisonment.

In addition, the book covers topics such as the selection of counsel, management of that relationship, and ways to mitigate or avoid litigation. The book is a reference to be consulted again as each stage of the process unfolds.

The practical perspective taken by this book permits company executives, managers, and many in-house lawyers to team up more effectively with their outside counsel counterparts.

In doing this, they will increase their probability of success up to and along the litigation path, all the way through trial. They will also create more possibilities for settlement, better settlements, and lower costs.

What This Book Is Not Designed For

Don't try this at home. This book is not designed to tell anyone how to litigate and try a case themselves. It is not nearly detailed enough to apply to any particular case. Instead, it seeks to enhance the experience of managing litigation and make working with one's litigator or trial lawyer a more meaningful and satisfying experience.

This book is not intended for seasoned litigators either, but junior litigators may find it helpful.

Finally, this book is not for smart-aleck opposing counsel to fuss over minor details or pluck my statements out of context to use against me in the next case. I have kept the discussion at a high level to make it broadly accessible. Making it more detailed would just mean another book that no one but lawyers will want to read. Plus it is this kind of pedantry that makes us lawyers unpopular.

If you find that this book is not for you for whatever reason, or at whatever point, I encourage you to send it back for a full refund.

Now Is the Time: Jump In!

You should not be dreading a dull read, feeling intimidated, or engaging in other excuse making. The common-sense approach in this book will immediately begin changing the way you look at litigation and the risks and opportunities it presents.

Whether your company is in the middle of a litigation right now, trying to avoid it, or is unlikely to find itself in litigation because you are proactively trying to minimize risk, this book will help you achieve your goals.

If you wait, you will not enjoy the many benefits that having a deeper understanding of litigation can give you, including achieving greater efficiency and cost effectiveness for your company, whether it is engaged in, contemplating, or so far successfully avoiding litigation. Don't let this happen to you!

It is time to jump into the black box and start unpacking it.

CHAPTER TWO

THE PLAYING FIELD

First, you need to understand the environment in which litigation takes place: the U.S. court system and its alternatives and the unique risk dynamics inherent to the litigation process.

The Federal System

In the United States, federal courts and state courts govern civil matters.

> In the U.S., **federal** refers to the procedure, substantive law, and court systems that govern the whole country.
>
> **State** refers to the procedure, substantive law, and court systems that govern within a state.

The District Courts Are Where the Action Happens in Federal Court

In the federal system, there are ninety-four federal trial courts, called U.S. district courts. The district courts have jurisdiction over two types of cases:

> (1) cases that involve a "federal question," meaning a question of U.S. federal law, such as RICO

> (2) cases that involve "diverse" parties: individuals or entities that are citizens of two different states.

Cases in which jurisdiction is based on diversity must also have an amount in dispute exceeding $75,000.

Cases in the district courts may be tried—meaning the evidence is taken from witnesses and documents, etc.—to a jury or to a judge, depending on the type of claim.

Certain issues in a proceeding may be decided by the presiding judge. These issues are questions of law and equity. Others are decided by the jury. This is called fact-finding.

District Court Decisions Are Appealed to the Circuits or to the Supreme Court

Decisions from the district courts may be appealed to one of the thirteen U.S. circuit courts. Twelve of the U.S. circuit courts—cleverly named First Circuit, Second Circuit, etc.—are regional, and decisions may be appealed to each of them from district courts within their respective circuit. These regional circuits may also hear appeals from federal administrative agencies.

The thirteenth circuit is the Federal Circuit, which has nationwide jurisdiction but is limited to appeals in certain types of cases, such as patent cases, or from certain specialized courts like the International Trade Commission.

The circuits are not trial courts and do not see the witnesses. Instead, they are appellate courts, and they consider the existing record: the exhibits that were admitted, the trial testimony, the submissions by the parties, and the court's rulings. Based on that official record, they determine only whether the district court applied the law correctly.

The Supreme Court is the highest court in the United States. Cases may be appealed from the circuit courts to the Supreme Court in the federal system. Appeals from the highest court in each state can also be appealed to the Supreme Court, but it takes only about two percent of the cases submitted to it for review. The Court has discretion to select the cases and issues it believes are most impactful. This is called "granting certiorari" or "granting cert."

The U.S. Supreme Court has a few other specialized functions. It may hear cases on appeal to determine the constitutionality of laws passed by the legislature and of executive acts. It can also interpret issues of federal law, such as cases involving treaties.

Finally, it acts as a trial court over a few limited types of matters, such as disputes between two states or disputes involving ambassadors.

State Systems

The state court systems are similarly structured to those of the federal court, with a trial court level and, in almost all cases, two appellate levels above that level.

The courts are called different things in different states, making it necessary to go past labels and review the function of these courts to understand what they do.

For example, the trial court in California is called "Superior Court," and the highest court of the state is the "Supreme Court." The trial court in New York is the "Supreme Court," and the highest court of the state is the "Court of Appeals." And in Pennsylvania, the trial court is called the "Court of Common Pleas," and the highest court of the state is the "Supreme Court."

The state courts handle approximately thirty times the number of cases that the federal courts handle each year.

Many states have a variety of other court designations as well, for example, small claims courts, municipal courts, traffic courts, courts of claims, surrogate's court, family court, housing court, probate court, and the like. These courts specialize in particular types of cases or issues, like divorces, traffic tickets, or landlord-tenant issues.

Often these courts have specific or streamlined procedures designed to resolve the types of cases they handle. Those procedures may employ certain variations or limitations of some of the procedures discussed in this book. Because business litigation is not typically resolved in these courts, I won't discuss them further, but you should know they are out there.

Judges and Juries

Judges in the federal court system are nominated by the President and confirmed by the Senate. They typically serve for life. Judges in the state court system may be elected or appointed, and they can hold their position for a certain number of years, or they may hold it for life. Whereas, juries in civil cases are drawn from the community and serve for that case only.

Equity, The Law's Softer Cousin

To understand the respective roles of judge and jury in business cases, it helps to take a step back and discuss the distinction between law and equity for a moment.

Historically, courts of law dealt with rules and statutes and rendered decisions based on comparisons to how similar cases were decided before. This provided a more or less consistent and predictable application of the rules across similar situations.

Foreseeable outcomes based on established rules of law promote harmony and grow economies. In contrast, think about countries which lack a significant body of case law, rules to enforce rights to intellectual property, or transparent courts.

This common application of the laws became known as the common law.

In the Middle Ages in England, these courts of law rigidly applied the rules, which could sometimes produce harsh results. So some equitable doctrines and remedies emerged that were based more on fairness and less on strict legal precedent.

One equitable defense is "laches," which prevents a litigant who has "slept on their rights" for an extended period of time from enforcing their rights later. They are prevented from doing so because while they delayed, witnesses and documents have become less available or unavailable to their opponent to defend itself.

Similarly, "unclean hands" prevents a litigant who has engaged in unethical conduct in the lawsuit from having the help of the court.

While some of these doctrines may sound a little "twelfth century," they come up in business cases all the time. Unclean hands was a huge issue in one of my recent cases between Qualcomm and Apple.

Legal remedies are typically monetary in nature. In contrast, there are three basic "equitable remedies," each again stemming from the common theme of fairness:

> (1) restitution, which restores to one party whatever they received from the other party

> (2) specific performance, which compels a party to comply with the terms of a contract where the promised performance was special or unique

> (3) injunction, which makes a party stop doing something they're doing, like using someone else's trademark without permission.

The Judge Decides Equitable Issues

In the United States, our trial courts are both courts of law and courts of equity. Most of them deal with both legal and equitable issues,[1] but the equitable issues are tried to the judge and not the jury.

Sometimes factual questions relating to the equitable issues may also help decide a legal issue. In federal court, the judge must decide the equitable issue in such a way that does not interfere with the jury's role in deciding the legal issue.

Some state courts, like California, take the opposite approach, requiring judges to decide the equitable issue even if it winds up taking away determinations the jury would otherwise make.

---

[1] Like everything else in this book, there are exceptions to my general statements. In Delaware, for example, they still have Chancery Courts, courts sitting in equity with no jury. Business cases are tried there all the time.

> Whether a company misappropriated another company's trade secret is a **question of fact**. There may be witnesses who disagree, requiring the jury to listen to them and "find" the fact.
>
> Whether it violated the law to misappropriate the trade secret is a **question of law**. What does the law say about this conduct? This is a question for the judge.
>
> Whether the misappropriation will be excused in this instance because the company who owned the trade secret led the other company to believe it had the right to use the trade secret is a **question of equity**. This is a question for the judge.

Timing

Overall Time-to-Trial

U.S. courts vary in average time-to-trial since courts have different caseloads and available resources, including the number of judges and clerks they have.

Federal courts are under pressure to move civil cases along, and according to data published by the U.S. courts on its website, time from filing to trial in civil cases can vary between about a year on the short end to three, three-and-a-half years on the longer end.

Trials can certainly go beyond three-and-a-half years, but most federal courts can get it done in that time. Of course, most cases are resolved in a way other than trial (dismissal, summary judgment, settlement, etc.) so time-to-trial is in most cases just a benchmark aiding comparison.

State courts vary significantly also. The National Center for State Courts, with the cooperation of the ABA and others, developed "The Model Time Standards" as a goal for state courts in 2011. According to the standards, time from filing to trial for civil cases should take about eighteen months.

Deadlines and What They Mean to You

Deadlines are a way of life for litigators. Deadlines are created by the rules and also by the court, and they dictate the timing of basic pleadings, discovery and responses to discovery, motion practice, pretrial activities, and the trial—pretty much everything that happens in a lawsuit.

Law firms have software that generates, tracks, and alerts the lawyers to the numerous deadlines in each case. The default timing of the rules for many events can also be modified, either by stipulation with the other parties and/or with the permission of the court.

Missing a deadline often can have significant consequences, so deadlines are taken seriously.

> Preparing work product with sufficient time for client review is key to managing stress for all concerned.
>
> A fulsome discussion of the merits of various options before creating that work product can save resources.

And since litigators often work on several cases at the same time, they tend to prioritize their workload based on the deadlines in their calendar. This means that the first time the client sees a draft of the lawyer's planned work product might be relatively close to the deadline.

For a client entity needing more time internally to review work product, it will be helpful to discuss that issue with the litigator so they can expedite the timing in which they will send drafts to the client.

More voluminous or more significant filings should also be given extra time for review and comment, whereas basic stipulations and the like will need no client review at all in most cases.

The Fluid Nature of Litigation Overcomes the Rigidity Created by Deadlines

Although the operation of deadlines creates a certain amount of rigidity, this is more than balanced by the extremely wide variety of tools in a litigator's tool chest.

The humble "notice of errata" is a tool that allows a simple correction in a court filing. It is more important to beat the deadline for a filing and file a correction than to miss the deadline and have it be perfect. Court filings should not be a reason for heart attack or stroke. However, this procedure is intended for small corrections, not because a new argument was discovered after the filing was submitted.

More importantly, if a court's ruling or a strategic decision creates a negative outcome or a missed opportunity, you can usually take advantage of that situation in more than one way and turn it into a positive outcome.

Good litigators should see—and create—opportunities all along as the case proceeds. Indeed, many negative interim rulings are not appropriate for interlocutory appeal because courts recognize that trial counsel can mitigate the harm from those rulings in other ways.

Transparency

Open Courts Are the Rule

One of the striking features of the U.S. legal system, from a comparative perspective, is its transparency and openness. Presumptively, court proceedings, along with the arguments and evidence being presented, are open to the public and to the press. This is a matter of constitutional importance for us.

This openness protects the integrity of the judicial system. The public can view how justice was administered and make sure it was done in a way consistent with our rules and precedent rather than in some arbitrary way. Since judges are aware that their decisions are subject to scrutiny from the outside world, the system is safer from corruption.

The Parties Can Achieve Temporary Confidentiality Protections

> There are a couple of different kinds of protective orders. The type being referred to here is an order entered near the beginning of the case that governs how the parties are going to treat confidential discovery materials in that case.
>
> Protective orders may also be entered for specific purposes, such as to limit the time a witness must sit for deposition, or to limit the number of requests for production that must be answered by a party.

In business cases, the parties can stipulate and/or the judge can order that dissemination and use of trade secrets and other confidential information will be restricted. For example, the parties may be prohibited from using materials designated confidential outside the litigation.

Often parties will then designate the bulk of their production as "confidential." Because the materials fall loosely within the designation, it makes it faster and easier to get their production out the door.

If something is over-designated, the adversary can challenge that designation, but that is time-consuming and expensive. The party defending the designation has the burden of establishing that the materials in question actually merit the designation.

If the parties settle the case, these items remain confidential. But if not, literally millions of documents may be designated "confidential" as the case approaches trial.

Luckily, by the pretrial phase, the parties will have narrowed the materials obtained through discovery to just those materials they plan to present at the trial. At that point, they will often be under pressure from the judge to remove remaining designations so the trial may be as open as possible.

On rare occasions, a court may hold a closed session around certain, truly confidential materials, but this is definitely not preferred.

Alternative Dispute Resolution Mechanisms

Neutral refers to an unbiased decision maker.

Besides litigation, other increasingly common ways to resolve a business dispute in the U.S. include arbitration and mediation before one or more neutrals.

Arbitrations Come in Several Flavors

Most business arbitrations in the U.S. are held under the auspices of the AAA (American Arbitration Association) or JAMS (Judicial Arbitration and Mediation Services, Inc.).

Arbitration may feature one or more arbitrators. Each of these agencies has its own set of rules, which may be quite similar to those typical in litigation, but the process as a whole is somewhat relaxed in comparison with court.

Arbitration is widely thought to be more streamlined, more flexible, and thus faster than court in resolving disputes, but this is not always borne out.

For example, arbitrators can be very busy people, making it difficult to change a hearing date without pushing an issue far out into the future, especially when the case is before a panel of arbitrators. Also, many arbitrators are former judges, so many of the discovery and other procedures are applied pretty much the way they would be if the case were in court.

Arbitration can be binding or non-binding.

Binding means the ruling of the arbitrator actually decides the case for the parties.

Non-binding means the ruling of the arbitrator is just advisory for the parties so they can consider the decision, but then decide the case in some other way if they want.

If the parties are sent to or agreed to binding arbitration during a pending litigation case, very often the court will stay the proceedings, meaning put them on hold. Once the case has been arbitrated, the court may enforce the award and render a judgment on it.

Judgment is the final, official decision in a case that is enforceable by a court.

Although in a non-binding arbitration, the determination of the arbitrator is advisory, the decision may be instructive enough—helping the parties understand the true dynamics of their case from an objective point of view—that they may agree to be bound by the decision. Or it may stimulate settlement discussions. If the case goes to non-binding arbitration, that may or may not stay or slow the underlying court case.

Unlike litigation in court, arbitrations are private and confidential, which is desirable for parties who would rather not air their dispute, documents, or testimony in public. This is helpful because it encourages the parties to be forthcoming in their attempts to resolve the dispute.

However, there are more limited grounds upon which one may challenge the decisions of the arbitrator(s) than one would have in court, and not everyone is comfortable with giving up those substantive appellate rights.

Substantive refers to the aspects of a case that deal with whether a claim or defense is or is not proven.

Procedural refers to the aspects of a case that deal with the procedures that will be used to determine the substantive outcome of the case.

The merits refers to the chances of prevailing overall given the facts and substantive law, and can be distinguished from purely procedural outcomes, like the application of the statute of limitations.

Mediation Is About Creative Compromise

Mediation is a process where no decision is made by the neutral. The mediator works with the parties to look past the positions they're taking in the dispute. The mediator focuses them on their underlying interests or concerns, and how they might find a mutually agreeable solution that meets those interests or concerns.

Thus, the primary focus of the mediation process is not the merits of the dispute—who is right and who is wrong under applicable law. That said, it is usually helpful for the mediator to have an understanding of the merits anyway. Understanding the merits enables the mediator to explain to each party why they are underestimating the risk or overestimating the upside of continuing to litigate rather than settling at mediation.

Let's say one's client is in a strong position, but the adversary refuses to see reason. It can be helpful for the adversary to hear why, from the mediator's objective point of view, the client is in fact in a strong position. The adversary will also know that a judge or jury might see things the same way if the mediation fails and the case proceeds to trial.

Similarly, if one's client is in a weak position but refuses to agree to a reasonable settlement, it may be helpful for them to hear the mediator's view that they are in a weak legal position. Sometimes clients discount what their lawyer tells them and need to hear it from someone else.

Courts and legislatures understand that mediation may result in an agreement that is more advantageous to one party than the other, but they believe there is value in the relatively swift and creative resolution of cases through the process of mediation.

Mediation proceedings are also confidential and inadmissible. Many U.S. jurisdictions even have a mediation privilege. This protects litigants from having their words in mediation—along with their communications involved in setting up the mediation—used against them later in court.

More generally, settlement discussions are usually inadmissible, although they may be discoverable in litigation. Compromises and other conciliatory statements are often necessary and useful to facilitate resolution of a dispute.

As a society, we want to encourage parties to make compromises and be forthcoming with one another without fear of having their statements used against them later in court.

Risk

An overview of the U.S. court system just wouldn't be complete without touching on some of the risk dynamics presented by litigation. Although many business endeavors involve balancing concerns about competitors, management, shareholders, public opinion, the environment, etc., litigation presents an additional and unique set of challenges.

Competition with a Hostile Adversary Requires Sophistication and Creativity

First, litigation features a hostile adversary, often one who has a relatively high level of control over increasing the cost and risks of litigation for its opponent. A litigant with a large litigation budget can perpetrate a great deal of expensive mischief against the litigant's adversary: bring unmeritorious motions, propound an oppressive level of discovery, and resist discovery by pushing every discovery issue to motion practice. Mischief can occur all throughout the case.

And even without mischief, litigation is an expensive process. Successful litigation requires legal research, fact development, careful analysis, persuasive writing, strategy, judgment, and the ability to recognize and take advantage of opportunities on the part of counsel.

In most disputes, there are facts that cut in favor of each litigant, so both sides have some merit. Even on points where there is a great deal of applicable legal precedent, every set of facts is somewhat different. Creative arguments are not only permissible but in many cases necessary to reach a robust result.

Judges and Juries Add to the Uncertainty

Second, litigation also features a judge making rulings throughout the case, some of which are unpredictable. Many rulings can have a significant impact on the litigation and/or on the litigants' budget. Pretrial rulings, such as on summary judgment motions, motions *in limine*, jury instructions, and orders on evidentiary objections can all have a profound effect on the ultimate litigation result.

And if the case goes to trial, some decisions will be made by a jury. Because cases are very often not black and white, even under the best of circumstances, the actual result may be a mixed bag or even a slam dunk going the "wrong" way.

> **Discovery** refers to the stage of the lawsuit in which the parties exchange documents, testimony, and other information.

Disclosure to an Opponent Is a Tough Bell to Unring

Third, U.S. litigation usually involves a substantial disclosure of information to one's opponent, such as a competitor. As we will discuss in chapter six, "discovery" is quite broad and permits an opponent to explore all kinds of information upon a showing of sometimes only tangential relevance.

Confidentiality and privacy concerns generally do not present obstacles to production of discovery materials to one's opponent. Courts consider protective orders sufficient to protect proprietary and confidential business information from improper disclosure.

For both parties, discovery can feel quite intrusive, distracting, and stressful. In many cases, it constitutes the bulk of the legal fees that must be spent.

Litigation Is for Keeps

Fourth, litigation can have lasting and significant effects, even long after the case is over.

Decisions and statements that must be made along the way should be carefully considered, not just in the context of the instant litigation but also in the context of the business.

Statements made in pleadings, discovery responses, motion practice, depositions, declarations, etc., are at the very least considered extremely probative. They may even rise to official judicial admissions that may not be controverted by later-introduced evidence.

Also, documents and deposition testimony disclosed by a party in one case may be subject to discovery in a later or other pending matter, even if the protective order in the first case prohibits direct disclosure of the materials outside that case.

The judge in the second case can simply order the party who produced it to produce it again. Or, more commonly, the former production is just "deemed produced," so it will be usable in the second case. This is called "cross-use."

The outcome of the case also may have a huge impact on the business. That impact may be direct and indirect.

Enjoined here means stopped by order of the court from doing something the party would otherwise be free to do.

For example, a party may be enjoined from producing a particular product, or from using a certain process, or from certain practices. Or it may have to pay a significant judgment.

In addition, many cases will involve findings or decisions that may be admissible in a subsequent case. Beyond the case, that ruling may have an indirect impact on the company's regulatory matters, investigations, international proceedings, and the like. It is also important for parties to take positions that are consistent with statements the company has made in other official contexts, such as in shareholder meetings or SEC filings.

Business litigants attempting to assess the risk of litigation must think broadly in the context of the business. They should also consider multiple scenarios based on possible rulings and the implications of those rulings.

However, litigation should be an opportunity, based on the same analysis, to consider those alternate worlds and think creatively about what opportunities arise from them. The work of clever lawyers shouldn't stop with a disadvantageous ruling.

Because of the many risks, challenges, and opportunities presented by the litigation process, the selection and management of counsel for the case is absolutely critical.

CHAPTER THREE

THE SELECTION, CARE, AND FEEDING OF LITIGATION COUNSEL

For best results in your case, you need to know what to look for in a litigation team.

Trial Lawyers Can Be Thought of as the "Seal Team" of Litigators

In most litigation matters, business clients will hire business litigators. Business litigators are lawyers who litigate disputes.

As we will see below, however, most U.S. business cases are resolved or settled before they get near trial. So while most business litigators have experience with attacking the pleadings, dealing with discovery, and preparing expert reports, many business litigators have never been to trial. This is true of even the heads of many litigation departments at excellent law firms.

That said, it isn't immediately apparent why hiring such a business litigator may be problematic for the client, since most cases do not get to trial.

Now imagine for a moment that someone tells your friend she needs to drive to some distant location; let's say, Chicago. She has a vague idea that Chicago is roughly north and very east of her present location and sets off in her car without checking a map.

Along the way, she will likely make a number of side excursions because she does not have a clear picture of where she is going.

Contrast the same friend who uses a map to plan out a route to Chicago. She might make a side excursion here or there. But she is more likely to make decisions along the way that are targeted toward her goal of reaching Chicago. Her decisions are more targeted, more efficient, and will represent less cost in the end.

Using Trial Counsel Focuses Resources and Yields Better Results

Since trial lawyers are familiar with trial, much like the driver who has a plan to get to Chicago, they will make better decisions along the way to increase the chances of success at trial. For example, they will:

- make smart decisions about which claims or cross-claims to bring and which might be problematic

- study the legal principles early on and determine who has the burden of proof on what issues and litigate the case with all this in mind

- develop a roadmap, or "framework of evidence," which reflects the claims and defenses and from which they will build a plan for obtaining the evidence that will permit them to meet their burden of proof or ensure their opponent fails to meet theirs

- consider and begin to establish trial themes early on so as to be able to take positions and make decisions throughout the case that will advance those themes

- conduct offensive discovery in a targeted way, spending their resources on what will matter at trial, rather than turning over every rock, regardless of relevance

- begin establishing their themes with the judge by persuasively explaining why the discovery they pursue is relevant

- establish their credibility with the judge by taking reasonable positions throughout the case

- have a plan for integrating the evidence that does not favor their client into their theme to explain it or mitigate its impact

- know how to prepare the case for trial, conduct the trial, and preserve the record for appeal

The benefit of using trial lawyers, and the discipline and focus this brings to litigation of the case, are well known and a matter of fact. My firm, Quinn Emanuel Urquhart & Sullivan, LLP, which is composed exclusively of trial lawyers, has had an overall win rate of almost 90 percent for more than a decade. This year, we were voted by independent research provider BTI Consulting Group as "The Most

Feared Law Firm In The World" in their *Litigation Outlook 2020.*[2] Opponents do not like to see us appearing on the other side of the "v" because they know we are focused, smart, and know how to win.

> Applying the discipline, judgment, and focus of a trial lawyer yields measurable benefits throughout the case, including swifter resolution, more advantageous trial and settlement results, and lower costs.

Trial Lawyers Enhance Settlement Prospects

Whether the case is likely to go to trial or not does not matter. Trial counsel with a plan, an understanding of the law that applies, and the facts under control has a great advantage.

They will often resolve the case earlier and more advantageously to their client than a business litigator who is dealing with one skirmish after another, and perhaps has not clearly thought through these issues.

Cases only settle when one's opponent believes it is better off settling than proceeding. So trial counsel that understands the merits of the case and is able to articulate them persuasively may be able to inspire the opponent to settle.

---

[2] BTI's decision was based on a survey of top legal decision makers at over three hundred organizations.

Alternatively, as discussed in chapter two, knowing the merits early on may help a mediator negotiate a mutually agreeable resolution between parties that may not be hearing the good advice of their lawyers.

Experience / Specialists

Some types of litigation, in my view, absolutely require a lead lawyer who specializes in a particular subject matter area. Family law is one such area.

However, most business litigation actually does not fall within this category. In most business cases, the benefit of having a trial lawyer—the targeted approach that comes from that discipline—is far more important than selecting a lead lawyer with specialized knowledge. As an example, technical cases have some parts that deal with the technology, of course, but most of the case will still depend heavily on the process and the substantive law.

Multi-Disciplinary Teams Bring Perspective

Many business cases require a team of lawyers anyway, so one or two of the lawyers with the needed background can assist with whatever specialized or technical aspects are in the case.

Indeed, it is a plus for some lawyers on the team *not* to have that background. After all, the decision-maker is a judge and/or a jury that does not specialize in that field either. Thus, the presentation must be organized and presented in an understandable way.

> Including skilled generalist trial counsel strengthens the litigation team by bringing fresh perspective and new ideas to the subject matter of the case.

Let's say you have a case that involves enzymes. A trial lawyer without training in biology often just learned about enzymes for the case; thus they may be in a better position than a specialist to know what someone just learning about enzymes would need to understand. They have looked at it with the fresh eyes of a newbie, just like those of the jury. They may pick up nuances or think of creative ideas that the biologist lawyer might brush over because their thinking is channeled somewhat by their training in that area.

Also, the generalists on a team likely have experience in a significant number of legal areas and can use strategies from cases in one area of practice in other areas.

Knowing really, really well how to reveal the truth in a way that is understandable to someone completely unfamiliar with what is being presented—a juror or judge—is truly a skill. The details of what the truth is in a particular case can be readily learned.

Existing Counsel Can Be Integrated

Sometimes a client has a close relationship with non-litigation or other litigation counsel, and they realize they need trial lawyers to prepare and lead their case. They can still use those lawyers, as existing counsel may have historical or other factual knowledge that is critical to the litigation. Good trial counsel can and should work cooperatively with the client's other lawyers to get the best results for the client.

Sometimes the client may want their existing litigation counsel to work side-by-side with trial counsel on the case. This is certainly very workable, but they need to give clear direction as to which lawyers are responsible for doing what.

It is also critical to have good communication throughout the team. All team members should be sharing relevant information, weighing in appropriately on strategic considerations, and working toward giving the client more service from the consolidated outside litigation team than it would get from the sum of its parts.

Nothing can be gained from making one's co-counsel look bad. Clients appreciate when their lawyers can play nice together in the sandbox.

Diversity and Culture

Let's say you're setting off on a treacherous expedition, and you can choose to bring five people who have the same tool kit as you or five people who have five tool kits different than yours. All other things being equal, which would you pick?

Of course, the group with the wide variety of different tools presented in the six different tool kits would be much more resourceful and resilient, having the tools to solve just about any problem they encounter. A trial team with a variety of tools will be similarly prepared for the many challenges presented by any case.

Now let's say the strangers you will encounter in your expedition all have different tools. The only way you can cross their territory is to show them you have a similar tool to theirs.

Again the six different tool kits will win. Similarly, the trial team with a variety of tools will bring multiple perspectives that may interpret the evidence in different ways, and in ways that jurors might also have after interpreting the evidence.

Diversity of Every Type Enhances the Trial Team

We as humans all come to the problems we encounter with our own skill set and life experiences.

Indeed, that is why we have the facts decided by the jury. We believe that bringing together a diverse group of individuals from the community—to listen to the evidence and the applicable law, deliberate with each other, and discuss their views on the evidence—translates to a more meaningful and just result.

More and more, corporate clients want to see diversity reflected in their legal teams. Many judges are sensitive to this issue as well. I remember as a first-year lawyer seeing six virtually identical young lawyers entering a conference room, and it was striking. They looked like robots; only the ties differed. Not so much anymore.

In addition to typical measures of diversity like gender, race, ethnicity, and the like, litigation teams benefit from having diversity of thought and analytical style and experience. Every member of the team brings different skill sets, experiences, education, and sensitivities to a litigation.

But There Must Be a Positive Environment That Encourages Participation

> Diversity is more than including different genders or different races or analytical processes on the team. It requires creating an environment where everyone can participate at their highest level.

Importantly, however, the only way to tap into this effectively is to create a working environment in which teams truly work as teams:

- Team members should benefit by supporting, not tearing down, their colleagues.

- Senior lawyers should be energized by, not threatened by, younger lawyers' ideas.

- Senior lawyers should remember how sharp they were as young lawyers and trust young lawyers to do meaningful work. This gets those young lawyers engaged, interested, and empowered to think and share their brilliant thoughts.

A good corporate legal team should be firing on all cylinders, with every member of the team motivated by the case and by their team members. They should be working cooperatively and sharing ideas to achieve great results.

A brilliant young lawyer that is fired up about their case can deliver magical results, and all the more so when everyone around them is fired up too.

Client Relationship and Good Communications

The litigation team does not end at the outside walls of the firm. The best victories often feature close integration and excellent communication between the outside litigators, the in-house teams, and the client employees knowledgeable about the facts of the case.

This integration is beneficial particularly when it begins before, or near the beginning of, a case because trial lawyers must understand the business and other factual context in which the events of the case occurred. This integration facilitates that understanding.

> When properly integrated into the litigation team, in-house counsel and other client representatives can play a meaningful role on the team without overburdening themselves and other company resources.

Teams Should Be Structured around the Needs of the Case

Close integration is not difficult to achieve. For example, early on in a complex financial derivatives case, we divided the associates into "product groups"—credit products, rates products, securitized products, etc.

Those product groups were then paired with businesspeople within the client organization. Since they had worked extensively with those products, the businesspeople were in a position to teach the associates how the products worked, how risk associated with those products was hedged, the jargon used in the industry around those products, and the business roles involved with those products.

These legal/business product groups had weekly calls and meetings together and analyzed documents together. By the time document production came around, the associates understood the documents, could spot the ones that were significant, and could ask intelligent questions.

By the time depositions and expert reports came up, the associates were far ahead in their understanding of the products in comparison with the opposing litigation team. Throughout the case, they could easily gather and develop the evidence needed to rebut or explain the opposing counsel's arguments.

Not every case is big enough to support this kind of effort, but you can usually structure the litigation team to master the facts quickly and efficiently. Sometimes a client may be reticent to spend money early on in a litigation, but in so doing, they elongate the process and spend more because the case could not be developed and shaped early on.

Good communication between lawyer and client, and good strategic planning, can never happen too early.

Strong Relationships Are Important and Make Litigation More Fun

A good relationship between in-house lawyers and outside trial counsel can also benefit the team.

The more these groups understand each other, and each other's jobs, the more efficient their work together will be. It will be easier for them to share ideas and ask questions.

When something goes wrong, the relationship focuses the team's resources on finding a solution to the problem, and the team moves on. Without the relationships, team members wonder if they'll be thrown under the bus.

Also, being pals means more people to laugh together at the absurdities that inevitably come up in every litigation. Litigation has a fair amount of natural entertainment value.

Clients in industries that are likely to face many litigation challenges would be wise to develop relationships with good trial counsel when they are not facing litigation.

In-house counsel might ask trial counsel to work with the company on certain projects. For example, trial counsel might help create defensible document retention / preservation policies; they might make presentations to key employees on best practices in certain areas, like proper labeling; and they might give MCLE[3] presentations on recent

---

[3] Minimum Continuing Legal Education

developments in the law to in-house lawyers, to regulatory counsel, to HR personnel, etc.

All of these are opportunities for trial counsel to learn more about the company and its legal issues and concerns. They are also opportunities for company personnel to see trial counsel in action and learn ways to protect the company from outside threats.

Another idea is to hire a firm lawyer to work within the company's offices for several weeks or months. When litigation hits, trial counsel has a huge advantage in understanding the factual context of the business and the case, and knows where the salient documents and witnesses are likely to be found.

CHAPTER FOUR

THE PLEADING STAGE

Initiating a lawsuit requires an understanding of how the scope of the litigation is set.

Let's start by introducing a few basic terms:

Plaintiffs are the persons or entities that have sued.

Defendants are the persons or entities that were sued by them.

Parties refer to the plaintiffs and defendants in a lawsuit.

Adversary or **opponent** or **opposing party** refers to the party on the other side of the case.

Claims and Elements

A fundamental concept of the legal system is a claim, also known as a cause of action.

A claim describes a set of facts which, if proven to have taken place, entitles the plaintiff to an enforceable legal right, a judicial action in their favor.

> A **claim** describes a set of facts which, if proven to have taken place, entitles the plaintiff to an enforceable legal right.
>
> **Elements** refer to the facts that must be proven.

An example is breach of contract. Under California law, breach of contract requires a plaintiff company to prove that:

1. the parties entered into a contract

2. the plaintiff did all, or substantially all, of the significant things that the contract required it to do (or was excused from having to do something it did not do)

3. the defendant company failed to do something that the contract required it to do

4. the plaintiff was harmed

5. the defendant's breach of contract was a substantial factor in causing plaintiff's harm

If proven, the plaintiff would be entitled to damages meant to remedy the harm suffered.

As another example, fraud under California law includes the following elements:

1. That the defendant company made a material representation to the plaintiff company that a fact was true

2. That the representation was false

3. That the defendant knew the representation was false when it was made, or that its agents made the representation recklessly and without regard for its truth

4. That the defendant intended that the plaintiff rely on the representation

5. That the plaintiff reasonably relied on the defendant's representation

6. That the plaintiff was harmed

7. That the plaintiff's reliance on the defendant's representation was a substantial factor in causing its harm

The reader will note that some of the elements here can be thought of as factual conclusions or ultimate facts rather than individual facts. Each ultimate fact that must be shown is set forth separately and is considered an "element."

For some elements, this may be very straightforward and require one available fact or admission. Some elements may require multiple pieces of factual evidence before a jury could conclude that that ultimate fact is met.

An easy way to determine what elements are necessary to prove a legal claim is by looking up the jury instructions for that claim. In California, for example, all the basic ones are available on the internet: google "caci jury instructions" to find the latest set of California civil jury instructions.

A plaintiff must ultimately prove each one of the elements in its favor in order to win on that claim. By the same token, if the defendant can show that the plaintiff cannot prove, or has not proved, one or more of the elements, then it will prevail on that claim.

Just because a plaintiff could prove all the elements in its favor does not mean that it *will* win that claim. There are a number of additional things that it must show or prove in order to prevail.

For example, the plaintiff must show that the court has jurisdiction over the defendant; that venue is proper in that court; and that the plaintiff has legal standing to bring that claim, as opposed to the rights to bring that claim belonging to someone else.

In addition, there are a number of defenses which, if established, will prevent the plaintiff from prevailing. An example of a defense would be the statute of limitations.

Complaints

U.S. litigation typically begins with a simple "complaint" being filed in court and served on the defendant.

The complaint initiates a lawsuit by telling the plaintiff's story, identifying the claims the plaintiff is asserting against the defendant based on the facts alleged. It is served on the defendant to put it on official notice of the claims against it.

The Construction of a Complaint

Most complaints in business cases either begin with a preliminary statement that summarizes the key facts or it can skip that passage and begin by blandly explaining who the parties are.

I view it as a wonderful opportunity to get to the point. A strong preliminary statement tells the judge, in a page or two, what the case is about and why our client is entitled to relief.

Some judges even recommend a visual that can be referenced in later pleadings and briefs to remind them quickly about the subject matter of the case every time something is filed.

After this introduction, the complaint sets forth the facts intended to establish the existence of personal jurisdiction over the defendant. It must also set forth basic allegations showing the court has proper jurisdiction over the subject matter of the suit and is a proper venue for the case. These concepts will be discussed in more detail in chapter five.

Next the complaint will tell the plaintiff's story, set forth in numbered paragraphs. For example, in a breach of contract case, the complaint might start with the defendant approaching the plaintiff with a potential business deal.

- Why was the deal important?

- What were the goals of the parties in making this deal?

It will introduce or attach the agreement that was executed. The material terms of the agreement will be highlighted.

- What did the parties agree to do?

- Why were these obligations material terms in the agreement?

The complaint will then explain how the plaintiff in fact complied with its material obligations under the agreement, but the defendant breached its obligations.

- How do we know it did not meet its obligations?

- What did the plaintiff do to try to compel the defendant's compliance?

Finally, the complaint will explain in general terms the harm suffered by the plaintiff because of the breach.

- What was the impact of the defendant's failure to comply with its obligations?

- How much money was lost as a result?

- What did the plaintiff do to try to mitigate these harms?

Once the facts of the story are in place, the complaint will then identify the specific claims being asserted against the defendant. For each claim, it reiterates the facts that serve as the basis for each element of the claims.

Some of the same facts might be used to support more than one claim, for example, a breach of contract claim and a trademark infringement claim. Each claim will incorporate all the paragraphs in the complaint before it, but that is just a catch-all. A complaint should still spell out each element and how it has been met for each claim.

Very often, not all of the facts are known to the plaintiff at the time the complaint is filed. The plaintiff may also draw what they believe are reasonable inferences based on the facts that are known. The plaintiff typically signals uncertainty in the allegations by indicating that those allegations are being made "on information and belief."

The last part of a complaint is called the **prayer**. The prayer summarizes and clarifies the relief that the plaintiff is seeking. It may include damages, declaratory and/or injunctive relief—listing whatever relief the plaintiff is theoretically entitled to based on the claims. This is followed by the submitting attorney's signature.

Pleadings Provide Notice and Set the Boundaries of the Playing Field

Pleading is a noun and not just a verb. As a noun, it refers to the papers filed with the court that plead the facts, including complaints, answers, cross-complaints, etc.

Despite the fact that it is supposed to be limited to documents that contain pleadings, litigators often use this term to refer generally to motions and other briefs filed in the court.

The true object of a complaint—which in some courts may be called a petition or application—is to put the defendant on sufficient notice of the claims against it.

The complaint is intended to allow the defendant to investigate the claims and determine its response.

The defendant may challenge the complaint for either not clearly identifying what is at issue or for stating a series of facts that do not, if proven, demonstrate the violation of any law.

Often, but not always, discovery will not start until these challenges are resolved.

When the pleadings are deemed sufficient, the parties may begin the discovery process against each other in earnest. (Sometimes courts permit limited discovery to be initiated earlier than the settling of the pleadings.) This can happen either after some motion practice (see chapter five) or when the defendant files an answer instead.

Courts Vary in How Much Certainty the Plaintiff Must Have to Bring Their Claims

The courts employ a few different levels of specificity to determine how difficult it will be for a plaintiff to file a sufficient initial pleading and therefore (1) put the defendant on sufficient notice of the claims against them and (2) open the door to the discovery process.

> Complaints must be sufficient to place the defendant on notice of the claims against them.
>
> **Notice pleading** requires pleading facts generally with less detail.
>
> **Fact pleading** requires pleading facts with more detail.

The predominant approach in this regard is "notice pleading," which has been adopted in federal courts and is still used in many state courts. With notice pleading, a plaintiff may plead facts generally, without including every detail.

While it doesn't require all the detail, some really bare-bones complaint is not going to cut it. The plaintiff must at least "plausibly" allege a claim, meaning a claim cannot rely on unsupported factual conclusions for key elements. The plaintiff has to present some specific facts to ensure the story plausibly alleges a claim upon which one could obtain legal relief.

Alternatively, courts may require "fact pleading." Since it requires a greater level of specificity, it makes it more difficult for a plaintiff to bring a lawsuit. Illinois state is an example of a "fact pleading" jurisdiction.

Each approach has a benefit and a cost. Notice pleading makes it easier for people to bring and pursue lawsuits, including getting to the discovery process, which tends to favor the plaintiff, but it is expensive and time-consuming for all involved. Notice pleading means a defendant may have to answer to a complaint without the plaintiff having to do much investigation to support its complaint.

Fact pleading makes it more difficult for people to bring and pursue lawsuits, which tends to favor defendants. However, some legitimate lawsuits may be dismissed and some injustices may go unanswered. An entity that believes it has been injured but does not have all the facts at its disposal may not even be able to bring a lawsuit. Or it must do substantially more investigation to uncover the missing facts before filing.

Even with notice pleading, most courts, including federal courts, also require a higher level of specificity in pleading when alleging fraud. This is intended to deter allegations of fraud without sufficient basis.

Service: Champion of Due Process

Due process refers to fair treatment in the legal system. Due process is thought to have originated with the Magna Carta, which for the first time prohibited deprivation of certain rights without "judgment of their peers and by the law of the land."

Service is the delivery process through which the complaint arrives in the hands of the defendant. Each U.S. jurisdiction has specific rules about what methods of delivery constitute proper service.

The approved methods in each jurisdiction are approved because they are thought to provide sufficient due process to a defendant such that it now has an obligation to respond.

Imagine getting sued secretly and not finding out about the suit until after it has been resolved against you. The service rules are designed to protect defendants against that kind of hanky-panky. Adequate notice providing a meaningful ability to participate is a fundamental requirement of due process.

Sometimes the approved methods seem a little behind the times in that they do not include some methods, like email, that might be the most reliable, or only way, to serve a defendant in a particular situation. For example, the plaintiff may have been corresponding by email with the defendant for years and not know the defendant's mailing address. Email might be the only way to send something reliably to this person.

Fortunately, at least the federal rules provide for "alternative service." This means that on motion from the plaintiff, the court can order that some practical method of service that would not normally be regarded as sufficient is sufficient to constitute service on that defendant in that case.

Games over Service Can Waste the Defendant's Credibility

Sometimes individual defendants think they can avoid the lawsuit entirely, or at least drive up costs a lot, by evading service.

In this situation, it is helpful to send the complaint to them any and all possible ways. This way they have actual notice of the allegations against them, even if proper service has not yet been effected. Also, because it's been sent a dozen ways—with the defendant still complaining that proper service has not taken place—this shows the court they are evading service.

Judges can become quite disgusted with a defendant who has received actual notice of the lawsuit but is evading service. They recognize this drives up costs and wastes resources, including the court's. Most judges would prefer to see cases adjudicated on the merits of the lawsuit rather than on procedural games, so they make an order that stops the defendant from avoiding service. (Score one for the plaintiff!)

After Service of the Complaint Is Complete, Service Becomes More or Less a Non-Issue

A summons is a special notice provided with the complaint that gives the defendant general instructions about what it must do.

Note that a complaint and accompanying summons are held to a higher standard for service than other documents in the lawsuit that must be served. This is because once due process has been satisfied by the defendant being placed on proper notice of the lawsuit, it has at least some obligation to make sure it is receiving other documents that are served on it.

Those later-served documents will simply be served on the lawyer for the defendant. In many cases, counsel for the parties will agree that email service is sufficient. It is convenient and reliable and saves their clients money.

"Proof of service" refers to the document that is attached to anything served on the opposing party that attests under oath how and when they were served so that it can be proven later.

Answers and Defenses

The most basic responsive pleading to a complaint is an answer.

In many U.S. jurisdictions, the answer requires a paragraph-by-paragraph admission or denial for each statement in the complaint. This means in a paragraph where some allegations are true and some false, the defendant must admit the part of the allegation that is true and deny the rest.

It is also permissible to respond by saying that the defendant has no information or belief as to an allegation that would be sufficient to enable them to answer, and so they must deny that allegation.

Verified means verified as true by a witness under oath.

In some jurisdictions, like California state court, if the complaint is not verified, the responding party may file a general denial. A general denial disputes all of the allegations in a complaint, and certainly the material allegations of the complaint, all in one fell swoop.

Most Affirmative Defenses Must Be Asserted to Avoid Potential Waiver

Affirmative defenses provide a reason the defendant would prevail even if everything said in the plaintiff's complaint were true.

After the admissions/denials, the defendant must then assert all the affirmative defenses upon which it has the burden of proof, meaning it is up to it to prove that these defenses apply.

Common affirmative defenses used in business cases include:

- Statute of limitations: one or more of the plaintiff's claims are untimely and are barred by the applicable statute of limitations.

- Failure of consideration: a contractual obligation is not enforceable because the plaintiff failed to provide the promised consideration for a contract.

- Contributory negligence: in a tort case, the plaintiff did not act with the requisite prudence, such that it contributed to the injury it suffered, which may serve as a complete defense or limit the potential award.

- Failure to mitigate: the plaintiff is not entitled to, or is entitled to less, compensation for its injury because it could have avoided that injury in some way but didn't.

- Release: plaintiff may not sue on a claim because such claim was previously released by contract.

Many defenses are waived if not raised in the initial responsive pleading.

The most common equitable defenses—and these are heard by the judge—are:

- Laches: the plaintiff unreasonably delayed in bringing the claim and in so doing has prejudiced the defendant or its case. Unlike the statute of limitations, the root of this defense is fairness.

- Estoppel: the plaintiff cannot go back on its word. The company may not be heard to complain about something if it would be contrary to a position it took previously and someone else relied on that earlier position.

- Waiver: the plaintiff waived the right it is now asserting.

A few affirmative defenses are built around the idea that claims should only be litigated once.

One of these is *res judicata,* a defense that the asserted claim either was already or could have been litigated in a prior case. The court considers three factors:

1. whether a previous litigation raised or could have raised the same claim

2. whether the parties are the same as in that previous litigation

3. whether that previous litigation was adjudicated to a final judgment on the merits, as opposed to being settled or based on a technicality.

Res judicata bars a claim because it was either already litigated, or could have been litigated, in a prior case.

Collateral estoppel bars litigation of an issue when it was already resolved on the merits in a valid and final judgment.

In determining whether a claim "could have been" raised, the court looks at whether the potential claim was related to the same "transaction or occurrence" that was the subject of previously addressed claims. If the answer to these three questions is yes, then *res judicata* applies to bar the claim.

A second and related affirmative defense within this category is collateral estoppel. This is also called issue preclusion. When an issue of fact has been determined by a valid and final judgment, that same issue cannot be litigated again between the same parties in any future lawsuit.

For collateral estoppel to apply, the court must find that

> (1) the issue in both litigations is identical and must have been before a court

> (2) the parties are the same or closely related to those in the earlier litigation

> (3) the issue was actually litigated

> (4) a final judgment was rendered on that issue.

Unlike *res judicata*, with collateral estoppel, the issues need to be identical, not just arising from the same transaction or occurrence. However, the claims or even the lawsuits may be very different. Identity is only necessary with respect to the issue of fact.

Like *res judicata*, the issue had to be decided on the merits and not on a technicality. But in addition, the issue itself had to be implicated in the judgment.

There are dozens more potential affirmative defenses, many of which may possibly apply in business cases. Google "affirmative defenses" for more ideas.

Also, as you might have noticed, many affirmative defenses arise from common sense reasons why someone shouldn't be liable even if they are the subject of a complaint. As a defendant, if you have a pretty sound reason why you believe you should not be liable for whatever the plaintiff is complaining about, it may be an affirmative defense.

In federal court, certain technical defenses are waived if they are not brought up in the responsive pleading or motion to dismiss:

- Lack of personal jurisdiction: the court lacks jurisdiction over the defendant in this case.

- Improper venue: this case was brought in the wrong location, contrary to the venue rules.

- Insufficient process: the content of the complaint does not comply with the rules for process.

- Insufficient service of process: the plaintiff has failed to properly serve the defendant according to the rules of service.

Some Defenses Can Be Raised at Any Time

In contrast, the following defenses are not necessarily waived if the defendant fails to include them in an answer or pre-answer motion to dismiss:

- Failure to state a claim on which relief can be granted: the plaintiff has failed to allege sufficient facts which, if taken as true, would provide adequate basis for a legal claim.

- Failure to join a party required by Federal Rule of Civil Procedure 19(b): the plaintiff has failed to sue other parties that should be in the lawsuit pursuant to Rule 19.

- Failure to state a legal defense to a claim: the defendant has failed to allege sufficient facts which, if taken as true, would provide adequate basis for a legal defense.

- Lack of subject matter jurisdiction: the court lacks jurisdiction over the type of case being sued upon.

Counterclaims and Cross-Claims

Often in business cases, the party being sued has its own claims against the party that sued it.

For example, perhaps the parties planned a joint venture together, which fell apart when party A failed to make the required capital contributions to the venture. Then party A ran off with party B's capital contributions, which included valuable trademarks. Then party B made libelous statements about party A, damaging its business.

Party B, who made its required capital contributions to the venture, has a variety of viable claims against party A. These include breach of contract, possibly fraud in the inducement, trademark infringement, etc. Party A has counterclaims against party B for defamation and unfair business practices.

In such instances, the defendant in the original case, party A, has the opportunity to assert counterclaims against the plaintiff, party B. This makes the defendant a "counter-plaintiff" as well as a defendant, and the plaintiff a "counter-defendant" as well as a plaintiff.

These counterclaims may be asserted at the end of the answer, after the list of affirmative defenses, or they may be presented in a separate document. Either way, the counter-defendant will have to answer them, just as if they were the allegations of a complaint.

Cross-claims arise when a party has a claim against another party that is on the same side of a lawsuit. For example, let's say the owner of a building sued a general contractor and two subcontractors. One of the subcontractors believes that it did everything right and the harm being sued upon was actually caused by the general contractor. The subcontractor might file its own cross-claim against the general contractor.

CHAPTER FIVE

ATTACKING THE PLEADINGS

The scope of discovery in a case is determined by the scope of the claims that are "at issue," meaning those claims that have survived attack and are actually going to be adjudicated.

Before the parties get to discovery, which is a relatively expensive and invasive process, they have opportunities to challenge a portion or all of the pleadings against them.

Some of these motions can eliminate or narrow the case, and some may just slow things down a bit. Any motion practice, however, is relatively expensive, so these pre-discovery motions can add substantially to the cost of litigating a case.

It is also helpful to discuss these motions because it permits an examination of some of the other requirements—beyond making sure it has a meritorious claim—a plaintiff must meet before bringing suit.

Motion to Dismiss for Lack of Subject Matter Jurisdiction

Jurisdiction refers to a court's general authority to hear a case, so "lack of jurisdiction" refers to a couple of powerful defenses, lack of subject matter jurisdiction and lack of personal jurisdiction.

Subject matter jurisdiction has to do with whether the court is entitled to hear the particular type of matter before it. Very broadly speaking, the federal courts deal with two types of cases:

(1) those that include a "federal question"

(2) diversity cases

If a case doesn't fall in either of these two categories, it can be heard in state court, which has much broader jurisdiction. The state courts may hear business cases based on state statutes and state law, such as unfair competition, breach of contract, breach of fiduciary duty, fraud, negligence, tortious interference with contractual relations, and the like.

In many circumstances, a plaintiff has a choice whether to bring the case in state or federal court.

Removal and Remand:

Sometimes a claim may be brought in either state or federal court. If the plaintiff brings the case in state court, but one of the claims is a **federal question**, the defendant may remove the entire case to federal court within thirty days of that defendant (or, in some jurisdictions, the first of multiple defendants) receiving the summons.

The defendant seeking to remove must obtain the consent of any co-defendants before doing this, but it does not require the consent of the plaintiff, who obviously wanted the case in state court.

Any claims in the lawsuit that are not federal questions may stay in federal court with the federal questions, or they may be remanded (sent back) to the state court.

Federal questions are those that arise under the U.S. Constitution, such as someone (maybe even a state) challenging an ordinance prohibiting certain types of communicative conduct on the basis that the ordinance violates their constitutional right to freedom of speech; a federal law, such as a U.S. statute; or a treaty as to which the U.S. is a party. In business cases, patent infringement lawsuits, which arise under 35 U.S.C. § 271, and federal copyright infringement claims (17 U.S.C. § 501 et seq.) are common federal court cases. Certain bankruptcy and antitrust cases are also handled in federal court.

Diversity cases are cases in which the persons or entities on either side of the "v" are from different states or countries and the amount in controversy is at least $75,000. So a case in which $200,000 is at stake and the two plaintiffs are both citizens of California, but the defendants are not from California (one is from New York, and one is a citizen of Louisiana) would be a "diversity case."

Therefore, a motion to dismiss a case for lack of subject matter jurisdiction is going to address these rules. In federal court, for example, the defendant might argue subject matter jurisdiction is lacking because there is no federal question and because both the plaintiff and the defendant are citizens of California. The federal court cannot hear the case unless it is satisfied that it does have subject matter jurisdiction over the dispute.

Motion to Dismiss for Lack of Personal Jurisdiction

Forum refers to where the suit is brought, without regard to the propriety of that particular forum.

Forum shopping refers to a plaintiff's selection of a particular forum over other possible fora because of its perceived benefits to the plaintiff.

Another important jurisdictional attack deals with whether the court in the "forum state" has the power to adjudicate the rights of the defendant—whether individual or corporate—in the case.

The court is not concerned about whether it has personal jurisdiction over the plaintiff. The plaintiff chose the jurisdiction in the first place and, therefore, has conceded the court's authority to hear the case.

The court must have personal jurisdiction over a defendant. Otherwise, the claims will be dismissed against that defendant.

Personal Jurisdiction Depends on a Defendant's Contacts with the Forum

Personal jurisdiction can be a complex analysis. The court must determine that:

- the defendant has minimal contacts with the forum state.

- the "minimal contacts" must be sufficient such that it would not offend "traditional notions of fair play and justice" to make the defendant answer to, and have its rights adjudicated by, the court there.

- these minimal contacts must be "purposefully directed" toward the state by the defendant.

> Establishing **personal jurisdiction** over a defendant depends on the number and type of contacts the defendant has with the forum jurisdiction.

The number of contacts sufficient to assert jurisdiction over a defendant depends on the facts of the case. For example, when the lawsuit arises from the contacts a nonresident defendant has with the state in question, or when the quality of the contacts is very strong, fewer contacts must be shown in order to avoid dismissal. When there are some contacts but the claims do not relate to those contacts, the court will consider whether the defendant is "essentially at home" in the forum state. This requirement is critical because it keeps a defendant from being forced to participate in a suit somewhere just by virtue of random or attenuated contacts it has with that place.

For example, when the lawsuit arises from the contacts a nonresident defendant has with the state in question, fewer contacts are necessary. Similarly, when the quality of the contacts is very strong, fewer contacts must be shown.

When there are some contacts, but the claims do not relate to those contacts, the court will consider whether the defendant is "essentially at home" in the forum state.

The whole idea here is to keep a defendant from being forced to participate in a suit somewhere just by virtue of random or attenuated contacts it has with that place.

Sometimes there is an immediate and obvious connection between the defendant and the jurisdiction in which it is being sued. Where a defendant individual is a citizen of a state or where a defendant company does business or has its headquarters in that state, the federal and state courts of that state have personal jurisdiction over that defendant. Since the defendant has decided to take advantage of the benefits of residing in that state, they must put up with the drawbacks of residing there also—like getting sued there.

As another example, consider a nonresident corporation *A* that has merely entered into a contract with a corporation *B* located in the state. Corporation *A* does not do any business in that state, and the contract is not at issue in the lawsuit. While the contractual relationship might be very substantial from a business perspective, it might not satisfy the requirement of sufficient contact with the state. This is because the only connection corporation *A* has with the state in this case is based on where corporation *B* happens to be, when the focus of personal jurisdiction is meant to be on where the nonresident corporation has chosen to engage in its business.

What constitutes "minimum contacts" is governed by a significant body of case law. There are many different types and combinations of contacts that companies or individuals can have with a state.

Must Be Reasonable to Sue the Defendant in the Forum

The court is looking for some act or acts by the defendant that shows it "purposefully avails itself of the privilege of conducting activities within the forum state, thus invoking the benefits and protections of its laws."[4] So a company would more likely be subject to personal jurisdiction in a forum state in which it has chosen to sell its goods, even though it does not have an office there, than it would in a state where its goods have accidentally landed due to the acts of some other party.

---

[4] *J. McIntyre Machinery, Ltd. v. Nicastro*, 564 U.S 873 (2011) (quoting *Hanson v. Denckla*, 357 U.S. 235, 253 (1958).

In addition to the minimum contacts analysis, part of meeting the requirement that asserting jurisdiction will not offend traditional notions of fair play and justice is making sure that doing so is reasonable. The courts do this by considering a multi-factor test. This test considers and weighs the interests of the plaintiff, defendant, forum state, and alternative jurisdictions in having the case adjudicated in the forum state.

Many states have "long-arm statutes," which set forth specific scenarios where minimum contacts will be found sufficient. Typical examples are nonresidents who transact business within the forum, commit a tort within the forum, or commit a tort that causes injury in the forum.

Personal Jurisdiction Is Subject to Potential Waiver

Personal jurisdiction, unlike subject matter jurisdiction, may be waived. It can be waived in a contract ahead of time. Or a defendant can simply not raise the objection and agree to adjudicate the suit in the forum chosen by the plaintiff.

If a party fails to raise the objection immediately and appears in the case, the claims will go forward, as the court treats the party as having waived the issue of personal jurisdiction.

Motion to Dismiss for Failure to State a Claim Upon Which Relief May Be Granted

A **motion** is a document that seeks relief from the court. One is said to be "moving" the court.

A **movant** is the party who is bringing a motion. The party responding to that motion is the **non-movant**.

A frequent challenge at this stage is a motion to dismiss for failure to state a claim on which relief can be granted. This is a mouthful, but it is actually wonderfully descriptive. In California, we cut to the chase and call this a general demurrer.

A motion on this ground is just what it sounds like: if the facts pled don't work to satisfy one or more elements of a claim, the claim is considered insufficient "as a matter of law" and is subject to dismissal.

On this motion, the movant has the burden of showing the insufficiency of the claim, and the court must consider the facts alleged in the complaint in the light most favorable to the non-movant. This gives the benefit of every doubt to the pleader of the claim.

If the court finds a claim is insufficient, very often the court dismisses it without prejudice, meaning that the non-movant has a chance to amend the claim and try to cure the insufficiency. Many deficiencies are just technical and may be solved through an amendment.

In fact, in some jurisdictions, the plaintiff may amend its complaint once as of right—meaning without the court's blessing. Because of this, many plaintiffs will wait until the demurrer is filed so they know what flaws the defendant perceives before amending the complaint.

Sometimes the facts that are material to establishing a legal claim are truly deficient and amendment will not help. This basically means there is no remedy that a court can give for the harm the plaintiff believes it suffered because the necessary facts just are not there. The court can only award remedies where the law provides it.

> On demurrer, the non-movant gets the benefit of the doubt and usually at least one chance to fix the deficiency, favoring parties' ability to have their claims resolved on the merits.

Thus, motions to dismiss on deficient causes of action can narrow the scope of a complaint, which in turn narrows the scope of discovery and of any trial.

Giving the non-movant the benefit of the doubt at this stage, and providing opportunities to amend is intended to ensure that meritorious claims can be heard, or at least reach discovery, even if the initial pleadings are poorly constructed.

Motions to Dismiss for Improper Venue and for "Forum *Non*"

Even if the court has personal jurisdiction over them, defendants can still seek dismissal if that particular judicial district within the state is not connected enough to the suit or to them.

> **Venue** refers to whether the case is brought in a place with a logical connection to the defendants or to the case; whereas, **forum *non conveniens*** refers to whether the forum is actually convenient for the parties and courts involved.

Venue: Propriety of Judicial District

Venue generally refers to which district within the forum jurisdiction the lawsuit should be adjudicated. The suit should be brought in a district connected to the defendants or to the subject matter of the case.

> **Residence** is basically where a person is domiciled or a company has its principal place of business.

Using federal court as an example, venue is proper in a judicial district where one or more of the following is satisfied:

- Any of the defendants are "residents," if all the defendants reside in the same state in which the district is located

- A substantial part of the events giving rise to the claim occurred there

- A substantial part of the property that is the subject of the lawsuit is situated there

If none of these requirements are satisfied, then any judicial district where the defendant is subject to the court's personal jurisdiction is acceptable.

If a court finds that venue is improper, it can either dismiss the suit, or it can transfer it to a more suitable venue.

Forum Non: A Broader View of Reasonableness Than Personal Jurisdiction

A defendant can also move for dismissal based on "forum *non conveniens*," or "forum *non*" for short. As you might guess, it refers to whether the forum is convenient or not.

When there is a viable "alternative" forum for the suit, that is, the suit could have been pursued in a forum other than the one the plaintiff chose, the court then looks at a multi-factor test. Unlike the inquiries about the defendants that are used to determine whether the court has personal jurisdiction over the defendant, this test balances the convenience of the plaintiffs and the defendants, as well as that of the two jurisdictions being considered.

The court considers a series of public and private factors on a motion to dismiss for forum *non*.

The private factors are:

- whether there is significant burden to the defendant in the plaintiff's chosen forum

- ease of access to witnesses and other evidence

- interest of the parties in their connections with the respective forums

- the enforceability of a judgment

The public factors to be considered and weighed are:

- whether the trial would involve more than one set of laws and thus cause confusion

- whether the forums being considered would have juries with a connection to the case

- any local interests in having the case heard at home

- whether the trial will take place where state laws govern

On this motion, the defendants must show the forum the plaintiff selected is inconvenient to the defendants and an alternative forum is convenient to all the parties.

If the defendant prevails, the plaintiffs can re-file the motion in the alternative forum. Although it does not necessarily end the suit, this motion can still throw a wrench into the plaintiff's plan and make pursuing the case more expensive.

Process-Based Motions to Dismiss

The defendant can bring a motion to dismiss for insufficient process or insufficient service of process. Both of these have to do with whether the plaintiff properly served the defendant.

Insufficient process occurs when there is a deficiency with the paperwork, for example, where the summons did not include the right defendant. Insufficient service of process means the plaintiff got the paperwork right but failed to deliver it to the defendant, either at all, or according to the rules.

Motion to Dismiss for Failure to Join a Necessary Party Under Rule 19

We saw in the previous chapter how the concepts of *res judicata* and collateral estoppel are animated by the desire for efficiency and finality in litigation.

> Parties filing suit should be thoughtful and realistic about whether any third parties are necessary parties in the lawsuit.
>
> The key questions are whether proceeding without a party interested in the suit will either
>
> (1) negatively impact that party's interests or its ability to protect its interests
>
> (2) create substantial risk to the parties in the suit of being subject to additional or inconsistent obligations based on the excluded party's interest.

Rule 19, the "required joinder of parties," and similar state court rules about compulsory joinder, are also animated by these principles. The rule states that all the parties necessary for the court to provide complete relief should be part of the litigation.

If a party was not included in the lawsuit and the court could not provide complete relief, then it may need to be joined as a party to the lawsuit.

The court must also consider whether proceeding without a party interested in the suit will either

- negatively impact that party's interests or its ability to protect its interests or

- create substantial risk to the parties in the suit of being subject to additional or inconsistent obligations based on the excluded party's interest.

One can imagine, as an example, an action that seeks to vacate—meaning wipe away—a judgment that distributed assets to two parties. The plaintiff brings the action against one of the two parties but not the other. The other party's rights will be impacted by the outcome of the suit, but because they are not part of the suit, they have no opportunity to protect their interest. Joinder may be appropriate.

Where the motion to dismiss aspect comes in is when the joinder is not feasible. For example, let's say adding the non-party would defeat diversity jurisdiction. In that case, the court again considers a multi-factor test to determine whether, in good conscience, the action should go ahead with the existing parties or it should be dismissed. The factors considered relate to how much harm would accrue to the parties and the non-party if the action proceeded without the non-party.

Motions to Strike

Motions to strike are less favored than motions to dismiss, at least in federal court.[5] Under the Federal Rules, a motion to strike permits a movant to strike certain statements from the non-movant's complaint on the basis that they are "redundant, immaterial, impertinent, or scandalous."

Don't Squander Credibility on a Motion to Strike

Way more often than not, complaints contain statements that the defendant does not agree with. That is why there are lawsuits. The plaintiff is not required to agree with the defendant. It is entitled to plead its case, as long as it has a good faith basis for what it pleads.

> Motions to strike can be useful when they can actually narrow the scope of the action—that is, when they can exclude extraneous and impertinent matter from the pleadings.

So there generally has to be good reason for the court to actually strike something from the complaint. This is a pretty drastic action, and if

---

[5] Motions to strike may be of more use in other jurisdictions. For example, in California state court, a demurrer is used to remove an entire claim, and a motion to strike is used to remove parts of a claim.

the motion is not solidly grounded, the court may view it as a time-and money-wasting exercise.

As a couple of examples, striking redundant material usually does not seem worth the time or cost of bringing a motion. After all, whatever you're striking is already in the complaint somewhere else by definition. So such a motion, even if successful, is clearly not going to have a material effect on the scope of the case.

Striking immaterial allegations is not much better because in most cases, it is not going to change anything important—or it would be material.

Try to Limit the Scope of the Action

Striking impertinent or scandalous matter might be useful though. The scope of the complaint defines the scope of discovery. So it may be useful to attempt exclusion of topics that are not just immaterial but were put there by the pleader to create an uncomfortable and/or expensive "fishing expedition" into these extraneous matters later.

For example, in a run-of-the-mill business breach of contract case, the plaintiff might include allegations about one of the defendant's employees' prior, ancient, and wholly irrelevant criminal record. Let's say that this information has nothing to do with the dispute at hand. It was just included in the pleading to embarrass the defendant and create an incentive for the defendant to settle the case quickly.

In this situation, the defendant may move to strike this irrelevant matter. Although doing so will bring these allegations to the attention of the court, they are just allegations. And if stricken, the defendant avoids having the plaintiff explore these issues throughout discovery and into the trial.

Anti-SLAPP Motions

A little over half the states have special motions to dismiss based on what is called "anti-SLAPP" statutes. SLAPP stands for "Strategic Lawsuit Against Public Participation." A SLAPP suit is a lawsuit which is brought for the purpose of silencing parties that speak publicly, whether in a lawsuit or in the legislative or other public context.

The anti-SLAPP statutes provide a mechanism whereby a party that was sued on the basis of their public speech can readily dismiss that suit. Also, in some instances, they can obtain attorneys' fees from the party that sued them. Accordingly, the anti-SLAPP motion procedure deters parties from seeking to prevent others from being able to petition the government or the courts.

Rule 11

Rule 11 Sets the Boundaries of Permissible Argument

Rule 11 actually represents a fairly rare attack on the pleadings. But it has a powerful deterrent effect on lawyers and litigants pleading in federal court.

Rule 11 refers to the federal sanctions rule for pleadings, which ensures that the pleadings presented to the court are basically legitimate and legitimately motivated. The Rule includes written motions and "other papers" presented to the court.

Because the guidance for litigants provided by Rule 11—and any state court counterparts—represents a set of basic "boundaries" within which the case must be litigated, it is helpful to discuss it in detail.

Rule 11(b) currently states:

> Representations to the Court. By presenting to the court a pleading, written motion, or other paper—whether by signing, filing, submitting, or later advocating it—an attorney or unrepresented party certifies that to the best of the person's knowledge, information, and belief, formed after an inquiry reasonable under the circumstances:
>
> (1) it is not being presented for any improper purpose, such as to harass, cause unnecessary delay, or needlessly increase the cost of litigation;
>
> (2) the claims, defenses, and other legal contentions are warranted by existing law or by a nonfrivolous argument for extending, modifying, or reversing existing law or for establishing new law;
>
> (3) the factual contentions have evidentiary support or, if specifically so identified, will likely have evidentiary support after a reasonable opportunity for further investigation or discovery; and
>
> (4) the denials of factual contentions are warranted on the evidence or, if specifically so identified, are reasonably based on belief or a lack of information.

The Rule Governs Anyone Making Arguments and Filing Papers

In the preamble, note that the scope of the rule's application is not limited to filed papers but includes oral representations to the court.

Also, note that the rule is focused on those who actually file or make the oral representations directly to the court. This means lawyers and parties without representation and not represented parties.

> Rule 11 and similar sanctions deter parties from making false statements to the court while preserving and encouraging honest and zealous advocacy.

The Rule Is Designed to Permit Honest Argument with Imperfect Knowledge

The rule does not require perfect knowledge on the part of the person making such a filing or argument. It requires certification "to the best of the person's knowledge, information and belief, formed after an inquiry reasonable under the circumstances" (Rule 11(b)).

This is important because many "facts" are actually inferences. After all, sometimes facts cannot be confirmed yet because they are primarily or completely in the possession of the other party. This language is designed to encourage responsible, honest representations and recognizes that parties do not always have all the facts at the time of the filing or argument.

Creative and Nonfrivolous Arguments Are Permissible

Most of the subsections of the rule are pretty self-explanatory, but subsection 2 merits a little extra attention, as it summarizes the living and flexible nature of American law. Lawyers in the U.S. are not limited to making arguments directly supported by previous legal authority. They do not have to have a statute that addresses the situation or a case in which legal principles were applied to a similar set of facts.

Instead, lawyers are free to make creative arguments as to how the law should or shouldn't be applied. They may argue to extend legal authority to new situations. They may suggest modifications in how the law was applied on some previous occasion. They may even argue against applying the law where it applied previously. Lawyers can also argue for the establishment of "new" laws. And all of this flexibility is meant to be tempered by one undefined word: nonfrivolous.

This is not a difficult standard to meet. Most arguments can be supported as fairly addressing a reasonable new legal proposition based on existing law or on a logical extension of the law. In my experience, most lawyers have little trouble staying on the safe side of the argument. Once in a while, however, someone gets overzealous (or desperate perhaps) and crosses the border into dishonesty.

Rule 11's Safe Harbor Highlights Its Deterrent Function

A litigant who believes a party has violated Rule 11 cannot just run into court complaining about the offending party. Instead, it must put the offending party on sufficient notice of its concern by drafting a motion that "describe[s] the specific conduct that allegedly violates Rule

11(b)." The motion is not filed but instead is sent to the offending party. The offending party then has twenty-one days of safe harbor in which to consider the positions in the motion and either withdraw or correct the offending document or statements.

> Rule 11's twenty-one-day **safe harbor** period allows time for the parties to discuss the offending pleading and for any misstatements in the pleading to be corrected, assuming the facts permit.

If it is withdrawn or corrected—or in the situation where the plaintiff can explain why nothing was wrong with the filing in the first place—the motion does not get filed.

If the party threatening sanctions is not satisfied, the motion will be filed and the parties will go through motion practice (see chapter seven).

If the court agrees with the movant, the court may issue sanctions against the offending party, which must be "limited to what suffices to deter repetition of the conduct or comparable conduct by others similarly situated."

Punishments Are Proportional

Any actual Rule 11 violation is a very serious matter to be deterred. But the court is not permitted to issue some draconian sanction that effectively bars a client from court, for example. The rule is meant to encourage honest arguments, not to slam the courthouse door if one steps over the line.

The sanction itself is therefore also flexible. It may include nonmonetary sanctions. In fact, this is the only sanction that may be imposed where Rule 11(b)(2) is violated.

It may also involve orders to pay some amount to the court or to the movant, whichever is appropriate to satisfy the deterrent purpose of the Rule.

The prevailing party *on either side* may be awarded reasonable expenses, including attorneys' fees. This should deter parties from using Rule 11 to silence legitimate complaints. Rule 11 motion practice is supposed to be limited to situations where the movant truly believes a violation has been committed.

All in All, a Broad and Flexible Boundary Permitting Zealous Advocacy

Thus, while the arguments are contained by a boundary, the boundary is extremely broad and flexible. The real control on most litigation arguments is the adversarial process itself. The lawyer or litigant on the other side is free to challenge and argue against the positions taken by an opponent. Both parties usually stay well within the wide spectrum of permissible arguments.

> Receiving a threatened sanctions motion in response to an honest pleading signals desperation on the part of an opponent.

Moreover, the unique fact pattern of each case creates room for differing points of view of which legal principles apply and how they apply in that particular situation. Ultimately, the decision-maker will consider the positions of the parties and determine which is stronger. Since the weaker position will lose on the merits, both parties are motivated to make the most reasonable and most persuasive arguments they can.

Some states have similar sanctions rules intended to deter parties and their lawyers from being dishonest in their statements to the court. California, for example, has a similar rule called California Civil Code of Procedure 128.7, which has similar guidelines and its own twenty-one-day safe harbor period.

Because of the breadth of legitimate argument contemplated by the respective sanctions rules, these rules rarely need to be invoked and instead serve as a powerful deterrent.

Moreover, a blustery sanctions motion served in response to a filing—assuming that filing is well supported and well researched—may suggest desperation on the part of opposing counsel.

CHAPTER SIX

THE DISCOVERY BATTLE

Discovery refers to the process in which the parties exchange, or obtain from third parties, factual information relevant to the case, including documentation, responses under oath, and sworn testimony.

Discovery is usually the largest line item in the litigation budget. Since most of the evidence comes from discovery, lawyers must make sure they do it well. Many litigators don't give it enough thought and attention, making it a blunter and more expensive process than it should be.

Discovery done well can also provide opportunities to educate your judge about the case, your client, and the opposing parties and their counsel.

Preservation of Evidence

Before every lawsuit, a duty to preserve evidence arises, ensuring the parties have the evidence they need for the case.

Parties are required to make a diligent and reasonable effort to find and produce the information relevant to the case.

Failing to Preserve Can Become a Costly Sideshow

Since the scope of discovery is quite broad, any litigant should err on the side of caution in trying to preserve all items that relate to the case. Failure to preserve can have serious consequences, including adverse inferences and other sanctions.

One aspect of this is determining *when* the duty to preserve evidence attaches to the parties. Usually it is a formulation like: "as soon as a party should reasonably foresee litigation." In practice, parties should begin the preservation process when a dispute becomes apparent. Considering the negative consequences that can result from a failure to preserve, it's better to err on the side of caution.

As soon as a party should reasonably foresee litigation, it should be sending out a litigation hold and otherwise preserving documentation and other evidence related to the dispute.

Back when documents were just on paper, the preserving process used to be pretty simple. A client could just gather up the relevant materials and make sure not to discard them.

However, the advent of email, messaging, cloud storage, data retention policies, and similar technologies changed all that. Parties must become aware of all the places where information relevant to the dispute may exist and take active steps to preserve those repositories.

Many companies have automatic document retention and destruction schedules whereby certain electronic documents are deleted from their systems on that schedule. Those processes must be stopped until the litigation is over.

Litigation Holds Provide Some Protection

To ensure complete coverage, the company should, and in some jurisdictions must, issue one or more litigation holds.

A **litigation hold** is a fairly detailed memo sent to everyone in an organization that might have access to materials relevant to a litigation.

It typically has these components:

- Background and description of the case

- The timeframe the events occurred and what departments or people were involved

- The relevant issues within the case and what categories of information might be pertinent to them

- A reasonably concrete plan for implementing the hold: who will be in charge of the process, how long the information must be held, and how electronic repositories will be collected and imaged

- Instruction to preserve the relevant materials

As the case develops, new issues may become relevant, and the memo should be updated and circulated again. Also, large companies with people coming and going all the time may need iterative notices to ensure everyone is aware of their obligations with respect to preservation.

A party being told that requested discovery materials are unavailable may seek information about the opposing party's efforts to preserve: What did it do, where did it look, and what did it find? If those efforts were deficient, the party may bring it to the attention of the court.

If the opposing party took steps to ensure that relevant materials were preserved, it may avoid the application of an adverse inference.

An **adverse inference** refers to a negative inference that can be drawn from a party's failure to meet certain obligations. For example, if party *A* fails to preserve highly relevant documents, party *B* may be permitted to argue to the jury that that the contents of the documents must have been bad for party *A*'s case or else they would have been preserved.

Discovery Plan

Whether plaintiff or defendant, it is wise to have a good roadmap before you set off on your journey. Once the claims and defenses are settled, the case is "at issue." At that point, the trial lawyers will have researched the requirements of the various claims and defenses and learned about the factual background of the dispute.

The Discovery Plan Is Based on the Framework of Evidence

This is a good time for lawyer and client to reflect on what elements are required by those claims and defenses and consider what facts—what documents, what reports, what witnesses, what third-party testimony or evidence—will be necessary or helpful to prove those elements.

Some of this information will be in the possession, custody, or control of the opponent, or of third parties, and therefore will be the subject of "offensive discovery." Other evidence will be in the possession, custody, or control of the client, and thus will be the subject of "defensive discovery."

As we will discuss in chapter eight, parts of the roadmap may have to rely on opinion evidence. This must be developed with the help of an expert based on facts from the plaintiff, defendant, and/or third parties. Some parts of the roadmap may also be satisfied by undisputed or undisputable facts.

> The framework of evidence becomes a starting point for the preparation of offensive and defensive discovery and keeps the litigation team and resources focused on what is important.

Working closely with a client to develop the roadmap, or "framework of evidence," can be valuable. This activity may help the client to recognize, early on, that certain facts or types of evidence are helpful. The sooner the lawyers can identify the categories of relevant evidence, the better.

The Discovery Plan Should Include Offensive and Defensive Discovery Efforts

The lawyers must prepare outgoing requests for production, interrogatories, requests for admission, notices of deposition, subpoenas, and the like, based on what is needed in the framework of evidence.

It is definitely to their advantage to have already decided in advance what evidence they actually need to establish their claims or defenses. As the process continues, they are likely to discover other possibly relevant materials to seek, but this process helps to keep discovery targeted, relevant, and defensible.

Similarly, the lawyers must gather relevant documents from their own client. Again, having previously discussed what types of documents are relevant and what witnesses are likely to have had access to that information, it will be much easier to begin the collection process.

Litigators' Tool Chest for "Offensive" Discovery

Targeted, Organized Efforts Can Save Significant Resources and Be More Effective

Litigators have several tools for gathering evidence from the opponent. Like any tool, they can be used inefficiently, costing more than they should.

Wise counsel will carefully craft the requests to target relevant and discoverable information as best they can without yet knowing much about the types of documents that the opponent likely has. This means they may be somewhat overbroad.

The meet-and-confer process, described in chapter seven, can and often should be used to trim down the scope of the requests. This becomes possible when more information is learned from the opponent about what is or is not available.

As for timing, the sooner a party obtains the underlying evidence, the better. The merits of the dispute rely on the evidence, and an understanding of the merits is the key to resolving the dispute. This is true whether the resolution is happening at trial or at the settlement table.

It is often helpful to follow up on the initial set of requests with other sets of discovery. Information is learned along the way, and these subsequent sets take advantage of that information.

Also, certain tools are best used after other types of information have been received. So for example, a party may want to wait for depositions until after they have received and processed the opponent's document production.

The Scope of American Discovery Is Relatively Broad and Turns Primarily on Relevance

The American system is adversarial in nature. It relies heavily on a full exchange of discovery from each of the parties involved. Parties considering litigation should assume that any information *possibly* relevant to the dispute and within their possession, custody, or control will have to be produced to their opponent.

That the production contains a party's confidential, proprietary, or even highly sensitive information doesn't stop it from being discovered. Such information may be protected by the court's entry of a protective order restricting the use of the information produced. For example, a protective order can limit an opponent's use to that particular case. Or it can limit the view of the produced information to certain categories of people.

This does not mean that discovery is a free-for-all, although commentators from other countries often perceive it that way. The scope of discovery is driven in large part by the pleadings and, therefore, what is actually at issue in that case.

So requests reasonably tailored to obtain evidence that has a bearing on what is at issue in the case are generally fair game. Similarly, *evidence that is likely to lead to* evidence that has a bearing on what is at issue in the case is also fair game.

As a counterexample, consider discovery requests that deal with an opponent's sexual history in the context of a basic business dispute. A party issuing such requests would have to have a very good explanation for why those requests are relevant to that case.

The federal rules, as recently amended, focus on relevance and proportionality. Proportionality can be measured using several different factors. But suffice it to say, it would be more difficult for a plaintiff to successfully limit the scope of relevant discovery where it has put a huge amount of money at issue in the case.

Document Requests and Requests for Inspection

Document requests—commonly called requests for production or RFPs—are one of the most basic discovery tools. Document requests have two basic parts.

Document Requests Are Designed to Be Inclusive

The first section of the document requests is a set of definitions that permits the party propounding the discovery to define what it means by certain terms being used in the requests.

> **Document requests are intended to capture basically any recorded representation of language, including emails, texts, chats, tweets, recordings, voicemails, notes on napkins, notes on toilet paper, markings on physical objects, and more.**

The definitions, therefore, can expand or limit the scope of any request in which they appear. Some definitions can be appropriately extremely broad. For example, the definition of **documents** is usually something extremely inclusive like:

"Document" means any written, recorded, or graphic material of any kind, whether prepared by you or by any other person, that is in your possession, custody, or control. The term includes agreements; contracts; letters; telegrams; telexes; faxes; inter-office communications; memoranda; reports; records; instructions; specifications; notes; notebooks; diaries; plans; drawings; sketches; blueprints; diagrams; photographs; photocopies; charts; graphs; spreadsheets; descriptions; drafts, whether or not they resulted in a final document; minutes of meetings; conferences and telephone or other conversations or communications; policies; invoices; purchase orders; bills of lading; spreadsheets; recordings; published or unpublished speeches or articles; statements; microfilm; microfiche; tape or disc recordings; emails; texts; chats; and computer print-outs.

The term "document" also includes electronically stored data from which information may be obtained either directly or by translation through detection devices or readers. The term "document" includes all drafts of a document and all copies that differ in any respect from the original, including any notation, underlining, marking or information not on the original. The term also includes information stored in, or accessible through, computer or other information retrieval systems (including any computer archives or backup systems), together with instructions and all other materials necessary to use or interpret such data compilations.

Definitions like these—and apologies for taking two minutes of your life with that—should ensure materials will not be excluded from production based on their form. Relevant documentary evidence could be found in any type of document, and the opponent should not conceal such evidence just because it was handwritten on a napkin, for example.

Definitions that refer to the parties in suit, or other parties, are also typically broad enough to specifically capture any officers, subsidiaries, agents, etc., of the party. Often a party does not take actions directly but, in fact, works through these officers, subsidiaries, agents, etc.

Other definitions will be provided so the opponent responding will have difficulty avoiding the requests by claiming it did not understand the various terms used in them.

The second section of document requests is the requests themselves. Litigators trying to avoid the production of relevant materials can object to the scope of the requests. Or they can move the court for an order excusing their client from responding. Therefore, requests must be crafted to anticipate a variety of objections and to try and navigate around them, or at least develop a strategy on how to deal effectively with those objections.

RFPs are typically drafted before the parties know what responsive categories of documents the opponent might have. Therefore, the RFPs may be drafted broadly to make sure anything relevant is captured, but also be subject to overbreadth because they capture irrelevant materials too. The actual production can later be narrowed by agreement or court order.

A Party's Credibility Can Be Established or Lost in Discovery

Another consideration in crafting the requests is how the judge will perceive them if they become the subject of motion practice. Discovery can be an opportunity for lawyers to educate the court about the strength of their client's case. They do this not just substantively, but by taking defensible and credible positions, communicating that their client has nothing to hide and truly is the reasonable party.

Trying to defend obviously overbroad "fishing expedition" requests for materials clearly outside the scope of the litigation may not aid in establishing one's credibility as a reasonable party.

Responding to Document Requests in Business Cases Usually Requires Some Outside Assistance

Responses and objections to document requests in most U.S. jurisdictions are due about thirty days after they are served. In some jurisdictions, responses also need to be verified by a party representative.

Document productions—the documents that have been requested—are often furnished well after the responses and objections are served in most business cases. It takes some time to gather them, stamp them with confidentiality designations, and produce the documents.

Parties responding to document requests are required to make a reasonable and diligent search for responsive materials. Sometimes they need only search for some narrowed scope of the requests that have been agreed upon or ordered. Emails and document management repositories may need to be searched. Hard drives may need to be imaged and searched. Texts may need to be gathered from employees. The list goes on.

Because this is an important effort, some outside lawyers and vendors have become specialists in the collection and preservation of documents. Also, some large companies that have a great deal of litigation even keep a special internal staff to assist the outside lawyers in gathering information responsive to requests for production. Efficiently searching for and collecting relevant documents from business organizations is not a simple matter and often requires expert assistance.

Physical Inspections Are Available

Inspections of relevant items are also available as a tool for litigators. For example, in a trademark case, the products using the marks may need to be inspected by the lawyers for the opponent. In a design patent case, the draft and final designs might be inspected.

Parties in litigation should think about what physical objects would be relevant to the case and request them. Photography is generally permitted at these inspections.

> Physical items may also be inspected, photographed, and in some cases, scanned three dimensionally.

Interrogatories

Interrogatories (nicknamed "rogs") are formal questions served by one party to the other. They are designed to gather factual information from the other party and about the other party's contentions. Usually they are crafted by litigators and are specific to a particular case.

> **Interrogatories** require a party, subject to objection, to provide responses to questions under oath. In some jurisdictions, they may be used to seek information about the opponent's contentions as well as straight facts.

Some jurisdictions, like California, call these specially crafted interrogatories "special interrogatories," but also have standard "form interrogatories."

Form interrogatories have form questions that may be selected by a party to have the other party answer.

Interrogatories Require a Party to Pull Together Reliable Information for the Opponent

Interrogatories must be answered under oath. They are usually limited in number, at least as a default rule, because responding to them is relatively burdensome. In complicated business cases, however, the parties can either agree to additional interrogatories or the court can order them.

The response must be a complete answer containing the responsive information the party—which often is an entity—has within its possession, custody, and control at that time. It can be difficult for the entity to put together an answer its employees feel confident enough to swear to *under oath* when there are multiple sources of key facts within the entity.

Interrogatories often start with definitions. In California, defined terms are capitalized. Examples of interrogatories are:

- "IDENTIFY all the injuries YOU contend YOU suffered as a result of the wrongful conduct alleged against Defendant in paragraph 62 of YOUR COMPLAINT."

- "State all facts in support of YOUR contention that the 2018 AGREEMENT was breached."

- "IDENTIFY all persons with knowledge of YOUR allegations in paragraph 19 of the COMPLAINT."

- "IDENTIFY, with corresponding model numbers, all the ACCUSED PRODUCTS sold between January 1, 2014, and the present."

Litigators usually work with their client to prepare draft responses. Responses typically must be reviewed by a company representative for accuracy and completeness and then verified, meaning signed under oath. Parties are expected to provide complete and accurate answers to interrogatories.

The responding party may object to the interrogatories on all the standard grounds, which are discussed in a subsequent section.

Responses may be amended throughout the case as more information becomes available. This can be a voluntary process. It can also be a requirement of the rules or of the scheduling order in the case.

Contention Interrogatories Have a Notice Function

Interrogatory responses can limit the scope of a trial. For example, let's say a party is asked to provide information supporting its contentions. This kind of interrogatory is helpful to the party propounding it because it fleshes out the allegations. The response should provide a list of all the areas that require discovery in support of that contention.

At trial, let's say the responding party wants to introduce some new support for its contentions in the lawsuit that was not in its response. That new support is likely to be excluded.

Parties are not supposed to "sandbag" each other. American discovery intends to create an even playing field by providing all the relevant information, and the opportunity to challenge that information, to both sides.

Requests for Admission

Requests for admission are classified as discovery, but they do not operate as discovery. Instead, requests for admission seek to narrow the scope of the case by obtaining admissions as to certain facts or contentions.

Requests for Admission Seek to Narrow Issues out of the Case

The rules on requests for admission, also known as RFAs, are usually bundled in the rules with discovery tools like requests for production, requests for inspection, and interrogatories.

However, unlike the other discovery vehicles, whose main purpose is to explore and discover the relevant facts, an RFA is primarily to narrow the case.

When a party makes a formal statement that is material to the case against their interest, it operates as an admission—whether it is in response to a request for admission, in a pleading, or in sworn testimony.

Some types of admissions are useful because they cannot be controverted later by other evidence. Thus, they resolve factual issues in the case, dispensing with the need to gather other evidence on that point. Other admissions are admissible and probative, but they may be weighed against other contrary evidence.

> Requests for admission must be carefully crafted to force the responding party to admit something helpful. Qualifiers and vague language permit the responding party to make excuses as to why they cannot respond to the requests.

Requests for admission are just what they sound like: formal requests to the other party to admit to certain facts. For example, a request might be phrased as a demand, such as "Admit you assigned the '849 patent to Apple in 2018."

Ideally, the request is a short factual statement that would be difficult to quibble with. It asks the party to admit something it really has to admit if it is being honest.

In the Apple example, the word "assigned" is a legal term but has such a common meaning and is so widely used in intellectual property cases that a court would likely overrule an objection to it.

Requests for admission can also be an easy way to establish the genuineness of documents in the case. For example, "Admit that Exhibit 2 attached hereto is a true and correct copy of your birth certificate."

Poorly Drafted RFAs Are Pretty Useless

If requests for admission are drafted correctly, they can be very powerful tools. Drafters must think clearly about what the factual issues are in the case and what a responding party is likely to know and can cleanly admit to.

If requests for admission are not drafted well, and this happens all the time, they will include one or more qualifiers that provide the responder with wiggle room, and therefore permit the responder to avoid providing a useful admission.

Consider the following RFA: "Admit that Exhibit 2 attached hereto is a true and correct copy of your birth certificate which was ordered in 2007." Let's say the propounding party just wants to pin down the fact that Exhibit 2 is actually the responding party's birth certificate.

If the responding party does not know when that particular copy was ordered, they will not be able to admit the RFA, even though they agree that Exhibit 2 is a true and correct copy of their birth certificate.

Consistent With Their Purpose, RFAs Must Be Answered Cleanly

Responding parties have limited choices in responding. They are supposed to admit the request, deny the request, or deny the request because they lack sufficient information to respond. Objections are also possible. Parties are expected to make a reasonable investigation in order to respond to RFAs.

Some RFAs have teeth: if the responding party unreasonably denies a request for admission, then it may be ordered to pay the costs and attorneys' fees that its opponent had to waste in proving that matter at trial.

Depositions

> A **deposition** is when a lawyer examines a witness who must testify to the best of their knowledge under oath about facts related to the case.

Depositions Are a Critical Tool for Almost Any Business Dispute

Lawyers need not depose their own clients unless they need to preserve their testimony for trial—for example, if they are terminally ill. Instead, lawyers usually depose the opposing party's witnesses and sometimes third-party witnesses to preserve their testimony.

Depositions are typically attended—either physically or, increasingly since the coronavirus outbreak, virtually—by the witness, the witness' or the company's counsel, the examining attorney, and a stenographer who is taking down the testimony.

Often in business cases, the defending lawyer is actually representing the party employing the witness rather than the witness herself. If the employee is not subject to any threat of personal liability in connection with the case, then their interests are usually aligned with that of the company.

If so, the company's lawyer's representation has no conflict. But the witness should be aware that they are not personally being represented by this lawyer.

In most business cases, videotaping the testimony is appropriate and recommended, and so if the deposition is in a physical location, a videographer may also be in the room.

Client representatives and other lawyers usually may attend as well.

A deposition is a formal proceeding and follows a question-and-answer format. A standard deposition day is seven hours of testimony, though they are sometimes shorter. A reasonable number of breaks may be taken.

The lawyer defending the witness may interpose objections to the questions before the witness answers. The basis for objection is similar to those for written discovery requests described above. However, in many jurisdictions, the lawyer is not permitted to tip off the witness by stating the nature of the objection and must instead say something bland to preserve the objection—like "objection to form." Objections are stated in order to preserve them for adjudication later by the judge.

Depositions Are Primarily a Defensive Exercise for the Deponent

From the witness' perspective, depositions are defensive. Many lawyers say that a case cannot be won, only lost, at a deposition.

The questions in the deposition of a party's witness—called a **deponent**—are formulated by the opponent's lawyer and are specifically designed to capture admissions from that witness that will be helpful in establishing the merits of the opponent's case.

The examining lawyer may try to loosen up the witness by making the deposition feel like a casual chat. A deposition is not casual, and the testimony is binding on the witness.

For example, the lawyer may ask a question that is subtly phrased to draw a conclusion that would be helpful for the lawyer's case. It may include some inflammatory characterization, like "steal" instead of "take."

If the deponent answers that question with an absolute yes or no, the witness has adopted every characterization in that question, no matter how inflammatory or misleading it is.

Most deponents are not accustomed to this level of literalness in their everyday speech. Without even realizing it, they can tire from concentrating on the words in the questions all day long.

Also, they can be presented with documents that they may not have seen for some time, or ever, and are expected to answer questions about them.

Depositions are defensive in nature.

Because a deposition is a formal interrogation with every word being taken down, the challenge in deposition prep is to get the witness to actively listen to the questions all day and give truthful *and accurate* testimony.

Testimony is not truthful unless it is also accurate.

For all of these reasons, depositions are a relatively stressful and exhausting procedure for party deponents. For third-party witnesses, who usually have a limited category of facts relevant to the lawsuit, depositions are less stressful but still must be taken seriously.

Depositions Lock in the Opponent's Testimony

For all these same reasons, however, depositions are an incredibly important offensive tool for litigators.

Depositions are usually the one opportunity for an opponent to gather testimony from a witness before trial. Assuming the lawyer is a skilled questioner, the answers can lock in the opponent on important issues in the case. The opponent may not deviate from these answers later at the trial without getting impeached (that is, called out on it).

Depositions also allow the examining party to gather background and context and general information from the witness that simply is not available through written discovery.

> Having clear objectives for the deposition, as well as a specific plan for achieving those objectives, is critical for effective depositions.

Smart litigators will have clear objectives in mind for the deposition as they gather the relevant documentation and prepare their examination.

While there should be a plan up front, the examining attorney should be actively listening to every word of the testimony because they will be formulating follow-up questions on the fly based on what they are learning.

To make things easier, very often they have an electronic tablet in front of them that visually displays the questions and answers in real time.

Individual and Corporate Deponents

Depositions may be taken of fact witnesses and expert witnesses. Expert witnesses are discussed in chapter eight.

There are two categories of non-expert fact witnesses: percipient and person-most-knowledgeable. The **person-most-knowledgeable** is also known as a **PMK** witness or, in federal court, a 30(b)(6) witness. Rule 30(b)(6) is the rule around PMK witnesses in federal court.

Percipient and PMK deponents are subject to different preparation obligations.

A **percipient witness** testifies from their own personal knowledge. What they sensed themselves, what they personally saw, heard, said, tasted, felt, etc. A percipient witness is about the knowledge inside a person, even if they are an employee of a corporation that is a party in the case.

While a percipient witness is not required to review the facts before the deposition, in many cases, their lawyer may want to show them documents to refresh their recollection. This makes it easier for them to provide the information they have to the examining attorney.

The defending attorney may want to do this to ensure that information important to their case is elicited at the deposition. If the information is not provided in response to the examiner's question, then the questioning party may later try to exclude that subject matter from trial.

A PMK witness is an individual designated by an organization to provide the facts that the organization has on certain topics. The PMK testifies on topics designated in advance by the examining attorney.

PMK depositions permit the examining attorney to get an answer that is binding on the organization itself. The PMK vehicle was designed to avoid "bandying," where the examining attorney must depose each witness with relevant knowledge. Instead, the designated PMK witness gathers all the pertinent information from within the organization before the deposition so they can answer with the company's knowledge at one (or more) depositions as appropriate to cover the designated topics.

Adequate preparation of a PMK therefore often involves the defending litigator and witness interviewing several employees and reviewing all the pertinent documentation. This is often needed to gather and provide accurate answers as to what the organization knows on those topics at the deposition.

The witness will be questioned on what they did to prepare to provide that testimony, and if it is found to be insufficient preparation, the witness may have to be deposed again. The examiner may ask who the witness spoke to and what each person told the PMK.

Deposition Preparation Produces Better Testimony

For any deposition witness, depositions are a big departure from everyday life. Especially when the facts happened some time ago, it can be helpful for the witness to be re-immersed in the events pertinent to the case, enabling them to provide accurate testimony.

Further, the defending attorney should prep all deposition witnesses, as it is critical to acclimate witnesses to the procedure as a whole, which is a somewhat alien interrogation most individuals have not experienced. The attorney explains the procedure and the importance of listening carefully and responding truthfully and accurately to each question.

General preparation should include a discussion of ways that questions may be tricky or misleading, the need to take breaks when appropriate, and how to handle instructions not to answer.

Preparation for a PMK deposition will involve significant work by the lawyers, the witness, and others to gather and ensure the proper review of the information relevant to the topics. The deponent needs to understand that their efforts to prepare will be examined as well.

While many questioning lawyers will act casual at the deposition in order to get the witness to loosen up, the witness should not forget it is a formal process and fall into a relaxed conversational mode. When a witness is tired, off guard, and conversational, they may say something that could be misinterpreted or taken out of context later.

A witness can also get sloppy and include information not needed to respond to the questions that the examiner then uses as a launchpad for a new series of questions. When the deponent volunteers information to the examiner, they are doing the examiner's work for them.

> Preparation for a PMK deposition involves significant work by the lawyers, the witness, and others to gather and review the information relevant to the topics.

Often lawyers will prepare their key witnesses by doing a "mock" deposition. The defending lawyer will ask questions while pretending to be opposing counsel.

This gives the witness a feel for how the deposition will go and helps them anticipate the types of questions that may come up. The lawyer and witness can think about how to formulate truthful, succinct, and accurate answers to the questions.

In some instances, the lawyer may have a colleague "black-hat" the witness, which means subject them to a very aggressive grilling. This can be great practice, and sometimes the witness comes back after the actual deposition to say how much easier it was than the "black-hat" treatment.

Most Questions Should Be Answered, No Matter How Dumb

At deposition, witnesses generally must answer all the questions posed. There are just two exceptions. Even stupid questions may be subject to objection by the defending attorney, but the deponent still must listen to them and formulate and give a proper response.

One exception is where the question calls for information that is not subject to disclosure because it is protected by a privilege, such as attorney-client communications privilege or attorney work product. In that case, the defending attorney is typically permitted to assert that objection and instruct the witness not to answer.

Sometimes the question covers some privileged and some non-privileged information. In that case, the defending lawyer can instruct the witness to answer only if the witness does not go into the privileged material. Sometimes a break may need to be taken in order for the witness to talk to the defending lawyer and become clear on what part is privileged and what is not.

The witness typically must answer all questions posed unless the answers are subject to privilege or the questions are truly abusive and harassing.

That said, the witness has control over the pace of the deposition and also has control over their testimony, which they can affect by carefully listening to the questions, thinking about the questions, and providing careful answers that are truthful and accurate.

Another exception is where the questioning is abusive or harassing or where the witness has a legitimate confidentiality objection to assert, say, on behalf of an unrelated third party with which their organization has a non-disclosure agreement.

Instructing the witness not to answer on this basis is a little touchier. The defending lawyer is not supposed to interfere with the examiner's questions, so they'd better have good reason to instruct. And some harassing questions may appear innocuous to a judge considering the merit of the objection.

Often the examiner will rephrase the question. Or they may back off or initiate a discussion, on or off the record, between the examining and defending lawyers to craft a better question. But they can also stick with their question and bring the witness' refusal to answer to the judge. If the deposition is over and the judge rules the witness should have answered, the witness may have to appear again for deposition.

Therefore, before instructing the witness not to answer, the defending lawyer must be prepared to explain why the question is inappropriate and off-limits and be willing to defend that explanation.

The Deposition Process Starts with a Notice for Party Witnesses

Depositions of party witnesses, either percipient witnesses affiliated with a party or PMK witnesses, may be arranged through service of a **notice of deposition**. The notice sets forth a date and time for the deposition, the party taking it, and whether a stenographer and/or videographer will be present.

In the case of a PMK deposition, the notice will include the topics the PMK must prepare for. The receiving party may serve written objections to the topics in the notice. Those topics may be modified or carved down by agreement of the parties before or during the preparation for that deposition.

Subpoenas

The above discovery tools obtain discovery from parties to the litigation, whereas subpoenas are the tool used by parties to obtain discovery from third-party witnesses.

Subpoenas may be used to obtain documents, in which case they include document requests. They may also be used to obtain testimony by deposition.

The third party may be a percipient witness, or it could be an organization, in which case the deposition is a PMK deposition with the topics in the subpoena.

> Courts tend to be more protective of third parties than they are about parties to the suit.

Courts can be reticent to force discovery from third parties, especially if they have little to no connection to the suit, but they rarely mind burdening parties and party witnesses. Parties are thought to have acceded to the burdens associated with having the privilege of litigating their dispute in that court.

Typically, a subpoena must issue from a court local to the witness rather than the court where the case is proceeding. The deposition and production of documents called for may also need to take place in the witness' locality.

Objections

Objections can and should be made to any of the various requests and interrogatories described above. Parties can both object to the request and respond to part or all of it. Sadly, because objections not raised are typically waived forever, most lawyers over-object just to be extra cautious.

Boilerplate Objections Waste Money and Are Disfavored by Courts

General objections are two to three pages of basic objections included at the beginning of a party's response to written discovery. In essence, the party is objecting to all the requests in the entire set if they suffer from the various flaws identified by the objections.

These are then followed by **specific objections**, which incorporate the general objections by reference even though they were to be generally applied in the first place. Then the special objections address various specific aspects of each particular request.

If something is still redeemable about that request despite all those objections, then the party will answer it. But only after some preliminary language like "Subject to and without waiving any of the aforesaid objections . . ." This language makes it a bit ambiguous about whether the response is complete or limited to whatever scope was not objected to.

> Most litigators over-object to be cautious, a practice that wastes the parties' resources and is disfavored by courts.

The general and specific objections are called **boilerplate**. Boilerplate is standard language not tailored to any true or particular concern about the request.

For example, "The responding party objects to this request as vague and ambiguous, including but not limited to its use of the term 'assigned.'" Or "The responding party objects to this request to the extent it contains a legal conclusion." Often, boilerplate objections are made to clear requests that could just as well be answered instead.

This method has become standard operating procedure in many jurisdictions, and it has been recognized as a scourge. Courts disfavor the use of a boilerplate, and some have more or less banned the use of it.

This prohibition has achieved varying degrees of success. Litigators' instinct to avoid waiver of any right—no matter how ephemeral—is a very strong force indeed.

Of course, many objections are important—like preserving one's attorney-client communications privilege—and absolutely must be asserted to avoid waiver.

But some objections are more tenuous, and while the responding party can see the *possible* application of that objection to the request, it could equally see that the request is actually straightforward and could be answered without including a series of time-consuming objections.

Now, in fairness, the responses are often made at a time when the responding party's lawyer also knows little about the categories of documents or other information that fall within the scope of the request. They may not have enough information to make a more detailed objection, and they are certainly not confident enough about that knowledge to waive their objections.

Boilerplate Wastes Resources Because It Hides Whatever Is Being Disputed

The main problem with this approach is that it obscures the issue of what is and is not being produced in response to the request. Since the boilerplate objections are not tailored to the request, they may not actually apply to limit the collection of documents that are responsive to the request.

So the lawyers propounding the request must now talk with the responding lawyers to determine whether the boilerplate objections are just to ensure non-waiver or whether they are actually limiting the scope of production. Often the parties go back and forth for a while before they are clear about what is and is not being produced.

Some of this back-and-forth process is in fact necessary because many requests need to be narrowed anyhow.

But it could be a shorter and more effective process if the responding party is familiar with the documents being called for by the requests, knows what responsive materials should be withheld, and objects more specifically in the first place.

Typical objections to requests of all types include:

- Attorney-client communications privilege

- Attorney work product doctrine

- Not relevant / unlikely to lead to the discovery of admissible evidence

- Calls for or depends on a legal conclusion

- Speculative

- Vague and ambiguous

- Unintelligible

- Burdensome / harassing

- Calls for expert testimony / opinion

- Compound

- Already in propounding party's possession, custody, or control

Most **boilerplate objections** obscure the actual disputes existing between the parties and wind up wasting client resources on both sides in clarifying where the disputes are.

The merit of these objections depends on the request to which the objection is being asserted, as well as on case law in the jurisdiction.

Privilege

Privilege refers to discovery materials that are protected from disclosure to other parties due to established public policy reasons. In each case, we as a society have decided that for certain types of information, some important policy reasons outweigh any party's need for its disclosure.

Why We Have Privilege Against Disclosure

The two most common privileges in business litigation are the attorney-client communications privilege and attorney work product. The latter is not really a privilege but a doctrine.

Each of these privileges varies somewhat in their formulation across U.S. jurisdictions, but as usual, the general thrust of them is the same across jurisdictions. Both of these privileges can apply to testimony or written documentation.

The attorney-client communications privilege protects confidential communications between lawyer and client from disclosure to adversaries because we want people to speak freely and honestly with their lawyer when they are asking for or receiving legal advice.

If privilege against disclosure didn't exist, then people would not be honest with their lawyers. As a result, they would fail to receive applicable legal advice that might keep them from doing something wrong. Thus, we permit those confidential communications to stay confidential between lawyer and client.

Attorney work product doctrine prevents the disclosure of materials that reflect a litigation attorney's work done in anticipation or as part of the litigation to their opponent. We have decided that it's important for litigation attorneys to strategize and execute those strategies on behalf of their client without intrusion by the opponent.

There are several other privileges against disclosure. The physician-patient privilege and psychotherapist-patient privilege encourage people to speak candidly with their doctors and psychotherapists. Similarly, the priest-penitent privilege encourages people to seek spiritual guidance without fear of what they may say being used against them. The spousal or marital communications privilege is thought to promote marital harmony and trust by excusing spouses from sharing the content of confidential communications they had with their spouse. We have also been hearing a lot about executive privilege. This doctrine enables the executive branch to withhold information from the public when it relates to certain national security needs and other information that is in the public's interest to remain secret.

Privilege Must Be Asserted to Permit Challenge and Avoid Waiver

When otherwise discoverable information responsive to requests for written discovery is subject to privilege, the privilege must be asserted. The same is true when privileged information is called for by questions at a deposition.

In the case of documents being withheld on the basis of privilege, a log of all the documents being withheld and what privilege is being asserted is typically required.

> For large cases, clients should consider using technology to prepare privilege logs. In every case, thought should be given to how certain log entries might be made (by category or by document) and whether they should be made.

Logs include basic information about the withheld documents—date, description, to, from, ccs, privilege asserted, and the like. But they do not divulge the privileged content. The basic information included should be sufficient for a litigant to challenge the assertion of privilege.

In the case of testimony, the assertion of privilege by the defending attorney must be made after the question is asked and before the witness answers. The defending attorney may also instruct the witness not to answer the question—an instruction the witness should always follow.

These privileges, like other legal privileges, are subject to potential waiver and must be asserted in order to avoid waiver. Waiver can occur through disclosure to a third party, although there are exceptions for confidential communications with some aligned parties.

Intentional disclosure to a third party will usually result in a waiver. Inadvertent disclosure to a third party usually won't. This is a very fact-specific inquiry, and the facts cross a wide spectrum of situations.

A waiver can mean a loss of privilege as to just that one document or bit of testimony, or losing privilege as to *all* evidence related to the same subject. A waiver of privilege could be strategically significant.

Often business parties that do not get along suspect their opponent is withholding documentation on improper assertions of privilege. Therefore the applicability of privilege is subject to motion practice fairly frequently.

Privacy and confidentiality objections may be asserted, but they are not as broadly applied as privilege objections. For example, to avoid the disclosure of information that a party would find embarrassing, a lawyer may try objecting on the basis of privacy.

However, full disclosure is considered important to the adjudication of disputes. Thus, where the requested information is clearly relevant, the law tends to view any privileges of privacy protection fairly narrowly and will require the disclosure.

> Because the entry of a protective order governing confidential information produced in the case tends to eliminate privacy objections later, parties that know sensitive information may be produced should consider including a broadly defined "attorneys-eyes-only" provision.

The same is true of proprietary or other confidential business information. Generally speaking, the courts are not concerned with the safekeeping of parties' confidential information; they are instead concerned with dispensing justice, which favors fulsome disclosure.

Private, proprietary, confidential, and other sensitive discovery materials must generally be disclosed but are protected from broader dissemination by a protective order.

Protective Orders

Most business cases involve the entry of one or more protective orders that govern the disclosures of confidential and proprietary information in discovery.

Protective Orders Facilitate Discovery by Controlling Disclosure

Protective orders facilitate discovery by limiting how the produced materials may be used by the receiving party.

Some courts have protective orders that they recommend, or the parties may start with one they prefer or have used before in another case.

In either case, the parties will customize those protective orders to their needs. The parties will negotiate over the various terms until they can agree to something. If they agree on terms, the court will usually issue an order based on their agreement.

If they cannot agree, then the terms at issue will need to be briefed (see chapter seven). The court will order one side's proposed language or its own version of a term.

Having to litigate terms of a protective order happens more frequently than you might think. And way more frequently than judges would like.

The protective order, once entered, and including any subsequent amendments, governs throughout the case and afterward.

During the case, the parties may designate their confidential and/or proprietary materials, including documents, deposition testimony, and responses to requests for admission and interrogatories, according to the designations prescribed in the protective order.

In a typical intellectual property case, for example, the protective order may have two or more "tiers," such as confidential, highly confidential, and highly confidential-attorneys' eyes only.

Each tier typically has (1) a definition of the types of materials that are appropriate for each designation and (2) a list of the categories of individuals permitted to see materials designated using each of the designations.

Categories of individuals that may be given access as part of the rules for one or more tiers include outside counsel for the parties and their employees and staff, inside lawyers for each party, party representatives (or sometimes limited numbers or types of party representatives), court personnel, experts and consultants, mediators/arbitrators, litigation vendors, and third-party witnesses (usually with some additional restrictions). Designated materials are not subject to public disclosure.

Negotiating the Protective Order Should Not Become an Endless Discussion

> Every pre-trial motion can be an opportunity to set groundwork with the judge about the civilized and righteous ways of one's client.

While negotiating a protective order is not the most exciting part of one's litigation practice, it is often very important.

For one thing, discovery is likely to be blocked until the protective order is entered. A party resistant to discovery can tie the negotiation process up for months. It will niggle over various proposed terms, suggest variations of those terms, write letters back and forth, etc.

This can be an effective strategy. Most parties are aware that the court will expect the parties to negotiate a simple protective order, and they are embarrassed to admit they cannot do so.

This locks them in an endless, expensive, and fairly useless letter-writing campaign. It also permits the other party to avoid producing discovery for a long time.

> Regardless of the subject of the meet and confer, it will save financial resources for the parties' litigators to quickly arrive at compromises where possible and to quickly determine the parties are at impasse where it is not.

Most parties wish to work out a protective order relatively quickly and move on with the case. Such a party would be wise to agree to whatever it can comfortably and have a clear factual and legal basis for the disputed terms it plans to stand on early in the negotiations.

Once at impasse, that party can conduct a proper meet-and-confer process (see chapter seven) and move the court for relief on those disputed terms.

If the adversary is taking unreasonable positions on those disputed terms, the lawyer can demonstrate to the court the adversary's unreasonableness.

This situation can also permit a litigant to set up a theme that the adversary is resistant to discovery. Some litigants are actually known for their institutional resistance (you know who you are). This makes setting this theme up early on not terribly difficult.

CHAPTER SEVEN

EFFECTIVE MOTION PRACTICE

Effective, smart motion practice, including understanding when *not* to bring a motion, is critical to business litigation.

Because motions are the main way the parties obtain relief from the court throughout the case, it is important to understand them.

Motions are how one can:

- overcome resistance in discovery

- force the other party to stop doing something while the case is progressing

- dispose of—meaning, win—part or all of the case

- take care of more menial issues like scheduling conflicts, page limits, etc.

Motion practice is how the parties seek relief from the court.

Motion practice can be expensive and time-consuming, and so smart decisions need to be made around it.

The Basic Paperwork

A motion, sometimes called a petition, is a document that asks the court (or arbitrator) to make an order on behalf of the party filing it, known as the **moving party** or **movant**.

After a motion is filed, the party opposing the motion may file an **opposition** in which that party may respond to the points made in the motion.

After an opposition is filed, the moving party can file a reply, responding to the points made in the opposition.

All this is generally called **briefing** an issue.

Once these documents are filed—the issue has been briefed—the court may or may not hold a hearing on the motion.

The motion, which comes with or includes a notice of motion, involves a succinct description of what the movant is seeking from the court. The notice of motion announces when and where the hearing on the motion will take place and the basic grounds on which the request is based.

A motion must come with a "memorandum of points and authorities." This supporting memorandum of points and authorities, as well as the other supporting documentation that comes with it, is what lawyers casually refer to as the "motion." Another term for this bundle of materials is "moving papers."

Sometimes the motion, notice of motion, and memorandum are contained in the same document; other times they are separate.

> Motion practice and discovery are two main drivers of legal costs in U.S. litigation.
>
> Parties and trial counsel alike should put some effort into handling these stages as efficiently as possible.

The Memo of Ps and As Is Where the Rubber Meets the Road

A memorandum of points and authorities to support a motion is a document, usually between fifteen and thirty pages long, depending on court rules. It can also be referred to more colloquially as the "memo of p's and a's."

The memo sets forth the statutes, case law, and other legal authorities under which the movant seeks relief. It also describes the facts pertinent to application of those legal authorities. Finally, it explains how those authorities, given those facts, entitle the moving party to the relief sought.

Memoranda of points and authorities are generically called "briefs." And for added confusion, some litigators call them "pleadings" even though they are not pleadings.

Oppositions and replies are also memoranda of points and authorities, but since they are responses to the motion, no motion or notice is required.

Oppositions are usually the same length as the motion's memorandum. The opposition may challenge the facts presented by the movant and add facts that were omitted in the moving papers. Oppositions may also present additional or other legal authority and/or explain why the movant's legal authority does not apply as the movant suggested.

Replies are usually somewhat shorter than the primary briefs and are limited to factual or legal responses to the points raised in the opposition.

Because each document requires a thorough explanation of the relevant authorities, substantial legal research is often needed. Through this analysis of case law, parties can show why the requested relief should or should not be granted under the particular fact pattern presented in their case.

The Legal Authorities Provide Guidance to the Court

The legal authorities supporting the briefs are usually available to the court and will be cited in the briefs with a citation that permits the court to locate the case.

Where a specific proposition is supported, the citation will indicate where in the case one can find the support for the cited principle. This is called a **pin cite**.

For a fictitious example, consider *Jones v. Smith*, 37 Cal. 92, 97 (1932). After the name of the case, there is a number, 37, which denotes the volume of the official reporter—a book—in which the case appears.

Next they record both the type of reporter and the level of court, which in this case is the California Supreme Court, "Cal."

The 92 refers to the page of the reporter where that case starts, and the 97 refers to the page where the support can be found.

The last element is the year of the case.

Statutes, cases, regulations, and law review articles all have their own standardized citation format based on the Bluebook, a legal style manual. This convention enables any lawyer, clerk, or judge to readily obtain the authority cited. Many cases can be located today by googling the citation, in our fictitious example: "37 Cal. 92."

Sometimes a published case has similar facts that the lawyer believes makes it a particularly compelling authority in the current case. The lawyer will, therefore, spend a paragraph or two explaining the facts and circumstances of that earlier case and why and how its conclusion applies under the similar circumstances existing in the case.

Carefully and honestly worded **parentheticals** can succinctly show there is ample support for the party's view of the proper result in this case based on cases that came to a similar conclusion in similar circumstances.

In other instances, briefs may include "parentheticals." A parenthetical is a short quotation or description in parentheses right after the case identification. Parentheticals are quick summaries of, or quotations making, the key point in that case the lawyer wanted to draw attention to by citing it. Example:

Jones v. Smith, 37 Cal. 92, 97 (1932) (court found party decedent nominated as executor had standing in probate action).

In a glance, the parenthetical quickly shows what happened in the cited case that is pertinent to the point being made. When several of these are listed back-to-back in a brief, it succinctly and effectively demonstrates to the court the ample support for the proposition for which the cases are being cited.

Memos Must Provide Facts Sufficient to Show How Law Should Be Applied

Putting aside items in the court's docket, which may just be referenced by docket number, most facts are completely unknown to the court. The pleadings are just allegations, and the court does not know whether they are correct. Without appropriate evidence supporting a motion, the motion should be denied.

Proper factual support for a motion, opposition, or reply brief should be provided in **declarations**, **affidavits**, and/or **requests for judicial notice**.

Declarations and affidavits must be made under oath and with sufficient personal knowledge of the facts being related.

Witnesses furnishing declarations and affidavits may be questioned later about their statements made in these documents.

The affidavit or declaration brings the factual evidence to the court's attention. An affidavit is a somewhat more formal version of a declaration. The requirements for an affidavit or declaration differ in each jurisdiction.

The main purpose, however, stays the same. Each of these is a testimonial document in which a witness provides information under oath and penalty of perjury.

The facts in a declaration can be a narrative like a story. They may also attach and include reference to documentary evidence that should be presented to the court.

Any relevant fact that the points and authorities are relying on generally needs to be included in the declaration or affidavit.

The facts in an affidavit or declaration need to be within the affiant's or declarant's personal knowledge. Often a brief must come with multiple declarations, sometimes attaching multiple documents.

Facts may also be presented to the court in a "request for judicial notice," where a party literally requests that the court notice some already established fact. This is only possible when the facts are so well known or obvious that they cannot reasonably be doubted. For example, records and rulings from other courts or the weather in the city on a particular day are facts appropriate for judicial notice. Basically, the court can notice facts "that are not reasonably subject to dispute and are capable of immediate and accurate determination by resort to sources of reasonably indisputable accuracy."[6]

A request for judicial notice is usually made with a very short and unopposed motion presenting the material as to which judicial notice is to be taken and why it is not reasonably subject to dispute.

Proposed Orders Help the Judge Rule

Some courts require proposed orders as part of filing a motion, and many lawyers do it voluntarily even if the court does not require it. The proposed order can spell out the exact relief the movant is trying to obtain in a format that the court could sign if it finds in favor of the movant.

---

[6] Cal. Evid. Code §452(h).

Sometimes courts require the parties to send proposed orders in a word processing program format so they can easily make adjustments.

> **Proposed orders** should be carefully worded to describe the relief the party believes it is entitled to.

The Meet-and-Confer Process

Courts do not have time to respond to every disagreement between the parties in the course of a lawsuit. The litigants' lawyers are expected to be civilized and reasonable enough to work hard to resolve the easier disputes without involving the court.

Many disputes can and should be resolved without motion practice. This can narrow the scope of a subsequent motion. If a party wants to bring a motion, most courts require them to meet and confer with each other first and declare they have done so in the moving memorandum.

For a movant, the meet-and-confer process is a valuable opportunity to learn about the opponent's theory of the case and certainly about the opponent's sensitivity to whatever is at issue.

By proposing various compromises on a certain request, for example, a lawyer can gauge the reasonableness of the opponent's position. Through this, they can get a sense for the likelihood of a favorable ruling if the request were taken through motion practice.

Assuming they have some flexibility, the lawyer can adjust their position on the request, so in any later motion, their position appears more reasonable than their opponent's. The reasonableness of the positions involved will be measured against what the law provides.

For example, let's say a litigant has refused to produce a document under a privacy objection. Legal research may be necessary to determine the merits of that position, meaning whether the privacy objection would, in fact, permit the document to be appropriately withheld from disclosure.

By performing this research, the litigant may determine that its position is not reasonable and it should give in. Or it may decide its opponent's position is not reasonable, given the pertinent case law. It may conclude that position will not be supported if the court is asked to decide the question.

> **Meeting and conferring** is an opportunity to narrow the breadth of requests and the scope of any resulting motion practice.

Given the hostility that courts have to unnecessary motion practice, lawyers have some pressure to really try to work things out instead of declaring an impasse on the issue. Many lawyers, however, squander the meet-and-confer process by failing to prepare or by not making an earnest effort to compromise.

A meet and confer is usually more productive if both parties are prepared. A fulsome meet-and-confer letter that explains the potentially moving party's positions regarding the requests at issue can help to kick things off.

This is because it puts the answering party on notice of the purported deficiencies. By arriving before the meet and confer, such a letter provides an opportunity for the receiving party's lawyer to communicate with their client and see if compromises are possible.

> The meet-and-confer process should not be endless.

As we discussed in chapter six regarding protective order negotiations, a long back-and-forth with meet-and-confer letters arguing the points can get expensive and, at some point, does not advance the ball. Once the parties have truly reached an impasse on an issue, and assuming that issue is significant enough, it may be time to move the court for relief.

Discovery Motions

Disputes arising from the discovery process are fairly common and may result in motion practice. Discovery motions come in two general flavors, motions to compel and motions for protective order.

Motions to compel are just what they sound like: they are a motion asking the court to compel the disclosure of information from the opponent to the movant.

If the parties cannot resolve all of their disputes over their requests for production, RFAs, etc., during the meet-and-confer process, then a party can file a motion to compel. The motion sets forth the unresolved requests and explains why, under governing legal principles, the objections raised should be overruled and the production should be compelled.

Just like any motion, a memorandum of points and authorities must be prepared, along with supporting declarations or affidavits, and often a proposed order. The opposing party must prepare its opposition, with its supporting declarations and documents. There is likely a reply brief and perhaps additional declarations and then a hearing.

In some courts, the movant is also required to prepare a separate statement that lists each request being moved on, the objections to each request, and an explanation for why compliance should be ordered. The opposition will often then require a response to the separate statement that explains why, for each request, an answer should not be compelled.

The whole process usually takes at least a month.

Parties Should Use Judgment Regarding What They Move On

One can immediately see this is an expensive and time-consuming process. Too often it is needed to resolve garden-variety objections that could have been dealt with had the parties tried harder to compromise during the meet-and-confer process.

To encourage this, many courts enforce the meet-and-confer process. Courts will carefully review the declarations of the parties, find fault with the process, and send the parties back to discuss some or all of the requests among themselves rather than ruling on them.

Although the moving party has the primary obligation to meet and confer over any dispute it is raising, the responding party is not off the hook. The responding party dishonors the court when it does not operate in good faith during the process. And an irritated court will not hesitate to declare that both parties failed to meet their obligations to meet and confer on the issues raised by the movant.

Other courts will hold a hearing, then either go ahead and rule on what they can and deny the rest, or order a supplemental round of briefing on certain issues before ruling.

Letter Briefs Are Your Friend

Another way that courts have dealt with this is through the letter brief. This delightful concept may be subject to different requirements in different courts, in terms of length, timing, etc.

A letter brief requires the moving party to submit a summary of what is still at issue in a letter. The letter must be filed with the court before the movant files a motion to compel but after the parties have met and conferred to impasse. The letter is usually short, limited to say, two to four pages.

The letter still works like a brief because it is a short memorandum of points and authorities. But it is much less formal, and it does not require the preparation of declarations or other formal supporting materials.

The letter is signed by counsel for the movant. Any documents pertinent to the dispute may be attached as exhibits.

The court then permits the responding party to submit an opposing letter brief of the same length, usually within a week or so, after which it holds a hearing, which can be in person or over the phone.

By the time of the hearing, the judge knows the basic issues already. Thus, they can use their limited time to ask questions and show the parties which way they are leaning on the issues. They can also tell the parties to meet and confer some more.

If the parties have agreed, the judge can also rule directly on the requests. But usually, this is unnecessary. The court's guidance—or sometimes even a menacing look—goes a long way toward adjusting the attitude of the recalcitrant party.

> **Letter briefs** are like including the judge in the parties' meet and confer process. By teeing up the outstanding disputes for the judge, the parties often receive guidance from the court that can bring those disputes to resolution without the need for formal motion practice.

Of course, it does not always resolve all the issues. The court can also decide after some discussion that the issue is too complex to resolve on the spot and order full briefing. Or one or the other party may request leave to file a formal motion because it feels the issues are too important to resolve informally. It has a right to present all the legal and factual support before the decision.

Nonetheless, the letter brief will usually expedite the process for some proportion of the disputes that reach an impasse. And it does this with much less cost and delay and much less burden on the court's resources than a regular briefing. The court's resources are usually pretty limited and should be devoted to resolving more challenging issues.

Motions for Protective Order Seek to Avoid Disclosure

The opposite of a motion to compel is a motion for protective order.

Sometimes a party propounds discovery and the other party determines that complying with the requests would be extraordinarily burdensome and expensive. Or they might have concerns that complying with one or more of the requests would mean producing materials protected by a privilege or would infringe on some other serious interest.

In that situation, the objecting party may move for protective order. In it, it will explain the facts and why, under the relevant authorities, it is entitled to the order of protection.

Unlike the protective order discussed in chapter six, the protective orders referenced here are specifically targeted toward protecting a party from abusive or overbroad discovery. These protective orders may limit or eliminate certain requested discovery, or they can provide additional confidentiality restrictions beyond what is provided in the original protective order entered in the case.

Motions for Preliminary Injunction or Other Preliminary Relief

Sometimes a party needs relief early in a lawsuit because it will suffer irreparable harm if the court does not grant it relief pending determination of the ultimate outcome. It simply cannot wait through the discovery period and until a judgment on the merits because the continuation of the harm throughout the case would cause such irreparable damage that it absolutely must be stopped immediately.

The party can move for preliminary relief, which addresses the following issues:

- Imminent Harm: why it would be imminently harmed if the court did not act

- Threat of Irreparable Harm: why that harm cannot be compensated later through transferring money or some other remedy

- Balance of Harms: why it is more equitable for the action to be taken against the other party than the harm to the movant if no action is taken

- Likelihood of Success on the Merits: that it has a strong position on the merits of the case

- Public Interest: that the grant of the motion would support the public interest

Strong Facts Without the Benefit of Discovery Are Needed

The court needs to consider all these factors because it has no other information to go on yet. Discovery has not yet taken place.

The grant of a motion for preliminary relief seriously impacts the rights of the party against whom it is granted. That party does not have the benefit of receiving discovery or of a trial on the merits. So the court needs to have a solid showing in all these areas before it makes such a grant.

> An **injunction** is an order that prohibits a party from doing something it could do or that compels a party to perform some act it would not do, such as provide restitution to another party.
>
> Because such an order infringes on a party's rights without giving it the benefit of a full trial on the merits, the court must be very careful about making sure there are good grounds for the order.

Several kinds of preliminary relief are available: injunctions, writs of attachment, restraining orders, receiverships, etc. Parties needing immediate relief and having strong facts should explore these options.

Dispositive Motions

A very important class of motions are known as "dispositive" because they have the possibility of disposing of a case or a good chunk of it.

The default path, of course, in U.S. litigation is to have a full trial on the merits. Both parties will do discovery and sort through the evidence, complete their legal research, and eventually have a trial.

One way to dispose of part or all of a case is on a motion to dismiss. We discussed motions to dismiss in chapter five. Another way is to settle, but that is not always possible.

Beyond those choices, the only way to dispose of part or all of a case without going through trial is showing there is nothing for the jury to decide. The movant must show two things:

1. there is no dispute as to the material facts of the case

2. those material facts only lead to one possible verdict

A party has a few opportunities to try to make this showing.

MSJs Provide Relief When There Are No Genuine Issues of Material Fact

A motion for summary judgment, or MSJ, is the first opportunity a party has to demonstrate this to the court.

On a motion for summary judgment, a movant must prove there is no "genuine issue of material fact," that is, that the material facts are effectively undisputed and entitle them to judgment.

If the movant is a plaintiff, it must establish there is no genuine dispute on the material facts and therefore all the elements of its claim have been met.

If the movant is a defendant, then it must establish it is entitled to a defense by showing there is no genuine dispute on the material facts relating to that defense, or by showing there is no way the plaintiff can meet one or more elements of its claims.

When there is no dispute as to the material facts of the case and those facts lead to only one possible verdict, there is nothing for the jury to decide on that claim.

The facts of the case must be viewed in the light most favorable to the non-movant on a **motion for summary judgment.**

Motions for Partial Relief May Be Available

The scope of relief available on a motion for summary judgment depends on the rules of the forum—federal, state, or arbitration. In general, however, parties can seek summary judgment or summary adjudication on all the claims or some of the claims.

Parties can also move on defenses, which dispose of claims and key issues, like whether one party owes a duty to the other party as a matter of law.

The court can also grant summary judgment finding liability, and then send the question of damages to trial so the jury can decide it. Whatever is not disposed of at summary judgment is teed up for trial.

Non-Movant Gets Benefit of Every Doubt, Making Summary Judgment Difficult in Most Cases

On a motion for summary judgment, the facts of the case must be viewed "in the light most favorable" to the defending party. In this way, courts hope to ensure that parties get a fair and full chance to get their claims or defenses to the jury. If the non-movant can show there is any legitimate dispute as to the material facts, the motion will fail.

The timing of a motion for summary judgment is dictated by the rules of the forum, but there is often a deadline set by which such motions need to be brought.

One defense to a motion for summary judgment is that discovery is not yet complete. It may be that the defending party has not yet had the opportunity to gather evidence that would present a genuine issue of material fact. Therefore, the deadline for most motions for summary judgment is after the period of fact discovery.

However, sometimes a party has made a key admission that makes any other facts immaterial. In those cases, a motion may be made earlier.

The facts often sit in the gray area where there is a genuine issue of material fact, and so those cases are not good candidates for a motion for summary judgment.

Directed Verdicts Are Available When It Becomes Apparent That There Is No Genuine Issue of Material Fact

Let's say the judge didn't grant summary judgment or no one moved on it. But then, during the trial, as the facts are presented through witnesses and documents, the situation changes.

It now—or again—becomes apparent to the movant that there are no genuine issues of material fact on one or more claims.

> **Directed verdict** can be ordered when, after the plaintiff's presentation of evidence and/or again after the defendant's presentation of evidence, it has become apparent that there is no genuine issue of material fact on one or more claims.
>
> **Judgment notwithstanding the verdict** can be ordered where, after the jury has rendered a verdict, it has become apparent that there is no genuine issue of material fact on one or more claims.

The timing of this revelation might be after the close of the plaintiff's case, meaning after the plaintiff has made its entire trial presentation. Or it could be after the close of the defendant's case. This is after both the plaintiff's and the defendant's trial presentations but before the jury renders a verdict.

The party may then seek a directed verdict or judgment as a matter of law (JMOL).

The standard used to determine if there should be a directed verdict is basically the same as on a motion for summary judgment: Can the non-movant show the existence of a genuine issue of material fact or not?

That is still not the last bite at the apple.

Let's say the party has now brought and lost a motion for directed verdict, and the jury has ruled against that party. At that point, the party may renew its motion for a directed verdict in the form of a JNOV, or judgment notwithstanding the verdict. (The abbreviation comes from its Latin name, judgment *non obstante veredicto.)*

Again, the standard for deciding this motion is the same. But this gives the court one more opportunity to look at the question after the jury has rendered its verdict.

When the Jury Really Messes Up

When the judge finds that the great weight of the evidence was against the winning party and a prejudicial error happened during the trial, the judge has one more opportunity to take the case away from the jury.

This situation may be pointed out by the party losing the trial on a **motion for a new trial**.

As you can imagine, the courts are not keen on redoing trials unless there is a compelling reason to do so. So besides showing the weight of the evidence favored the losing party, the movant also must show one or more of the following:

- irregularities that prevented the parties from experiencing a fair trial

- some misconduct by the jury or by the opposing party

- some new or previously undiscovered evidence

- one or more errors of law

- damages awarded being wildly off in either direction

- evidence showing the jury did not follow the jury instructions

A motion for a new trial may be mixed with a JNOV. If the evidence is materially uncontroverted by a party, then a JNOV may be appropriate.

If the evidence is mostly for one side but some evidence favors the other, then a JNOV is not appropriate, but a new trial might be a possibility.

Administrative Motions

The motions discussed above are just the very beginning.

The court can receive requests, in the form of motions, for all kinds of basic procedural issues:

- Motion to exceed the page limit

- Motion to file a late brief

- Motion to file surreply (a reply to a reply brief)

- Motion for an extension of time on a deadline

- Motion for injunction pending appeal

- Motion to consolidate

- Motion to stay

- Motion to seal documents

- Motion for alternative service

- Motion to compel arbitration

Motions may seek an award of certain types of relief, such as motions for costs, for attorneys' fees, for sanctions, for constructive trust, and to appoint a receiver.

Motions are also the vehicle to use to seek changes of the status of a lawyer in relation to a party:

- Motion to withdraw as counsel

- Motion to substitute counsel

- Motion for disqualification

Note that in many instances, the parties may agree on the relief being requested and can stipulate to it instead. This eliminates the need to bring a motion. Just because an issue needs to be decided, it doesn't have to be litigated, and courts are usually pretty receptive to granting relief when both parties are amenable.

Motions for Reconsideration and Other Options for the Loser

The losing party on a motion has a few options.

Living with It Is an Option

One option is to go along with the ruling and/or figure out another way to go about whatever it was trying to achieve.

Maybe the party can propound narrower requests, get the information from a deposition, or subpoena a third party. Maybe it can move for directed verdict. Maybe nothing needs to be done.

Moreover, sometimes the court's ruling actually provides guidance into how the court sees the matter and generates new ideas about what should be pursued. Litigation is a flexible process, and losing parties should keep the loss in the proper perspective.

Reconsideration Is Usually Not Available

The other option is a motion for reconsideration, but this is an uphill battle. The last thing that courts like to see is a party coming back to quibble with their ruling. They do not permit a motion for reconsideration unless it is promptly filed.

> There are rarely good grounds for a **motion for reconsideration** since the movant must show new or different facts, circumstances, or law than what was known at the time the hearing took place.

Also, more importantly, courts require the party seeking reconsideration to show the motion is based on new or different facts, circumstances, or law than what was known at the time the hearing took place. Most of the time, this requirement cannot be met.

Interlocutory Appeal Is Also an Uphill Battle

Some rulings may also be challengeable at the appellate level.

Typically, most rulings must wait until the end of the case, at which point they can be raised in the appeal. But certain types of rulings may be brought up right away with permission of the appellate court.

In such cases, the party usually must show that if the outstanding issue is not addressed immediately, it will create extreme prejudice to the party seeking review. Also, it helps to show that the legal issue has broader application to the public at large rather than being peculiarly important to just the parties.

Bottom line: since none of these options are wonderful, it is ideal to win the motion in the first place. This means, besides having a robust meet-and-confer process and a realistic idea of the merits, parties need to generate strong and well-supported motion papers. Most motions are decided on the papers, whether or not there is a hearing.

CHAPTER EIGHT

WRANGLING EXPERT WITNESSES

In chapter six, the process we discussed was limited to **fact discovery**. In fact discovery, the parties gather and exchange the relevant documentation and testimony and written factual answers so both parties are operating from the same set of facts. However, most business cases have another area of discovery: expert discovery.

This chapter is important because in most business cases, the parties will require the assistance of experts to analyze and interpret the relevant information. They must apply their expertise to prepare an opinion about the facts that can be presented to the jury.

Some fields don't have many great experts, so even if it does not need the analysis until after fact discovery ends, it benefits a party to consider what expert evidence is needed early in the case. This enables the party to reach out to the expert before the other side has contacted them.

Expert Selection

Parties Should Consider Expert Opinion When Creating Their Framework of Evidence

> The framework of evidence prepared at the beginning of the case may call for required facts or opinion to be provided by one or more **expert witnesses**.
>
> In the American system, expert witnesses usually work for the respective parties rather than being hired by the court, though this is possible too.

In chapters two and six, we discussed the "framework of evidence," or roadmap, that the trial lawyer will put together at the beginning of the case. In the framework, they and their client will fill in where they intend to obtain the evidence needed to prove their claims or defenses.

Some of the evidence needed will likely come in the form of expert opinion.

For example, the case might involve determining whether the handwriting on a document is that of a particular person. A layperson's opinion on that matter is not reliable. In fact, true handwriting analysis takes years of study and practice.

Therefore, the party who needs the jury to hear this information may hire a handwriting expert. This expert will review the document and other known samples of the person's writing and develop an opinion, based on their experience and expertise, about whether it is or isn't the person's handwriting.

Sometimes the analysis is more involved and requires testing. For example, to conduct ink analysis of various types, small plugs must be taken from the document. The plugs are then tested for certain qualities. The ink chemist expert will then prepare a report or other presentation based on the process used to conduct the testing, and the result and what it indicated to them.

A very common area of expert testimony—in almost every business case, in fact—is in calculating the damages due to the plaintiff or counterclaim defendant if successful in proving its case. Depending on the theory being contemplated to prove damages, the party may hire an expert with an accounting background and/or an economics background as their damages expert.

For example, in a trademark case where the defendant infringed someone else's marks, the expert might compare the increase in their profit margin during the period before and after their infringement. After considering other factors that might have played into the increase, they will derive an amount that estimates the profits that should be disgorged by the defendant to make up for its infringement.

Or in a case where the defendant included in its product a feature that was the subject of someone else's patent, the expert might consider licenses for similar features in similar products. The expert will use these "comps" to calculate what might have been an appropriate license rate had the defendant licensed it, rather than infringing the patent.

The defendant or counterclaim plaintiff usually has their own expert that reviews and analyzes the first expert's report or testimony and explains why their analysis is wrong.

Who Can Serve as an Expert?

The test for who can serve as an expert witness is broad and flexible: anyone with knowledge, skill, education, experience, or training in a specialized field. The test needs to be broad and flexible because of the wide variety of facts that may need some level of expert analysis.

Ultimately, the jury will assess the credibility and reliability of the expert and their opinion just as it would any other witness. So the expert's credentials, analysis, and the opinion they render are all very important.

An **expert** will be disclosed to the opponent and is intended to provide trial testimony.

A **consultant** typically is not disclosed to the opponent but provides expertise behind the scenes to the trial lawyers and the client.

The reader will note that this chapter relates only to testifying (or potentially testifying) experts and not non-testifying consultants. A consultant helps the lawyer and/or a testifying expert behind the scenes but is not intended to ever take the stand. Often, consultants can play a role in helping shape and create expert analyses needed for the case.

Finding Suitable Experts

From the lawyer's framework of evidence, they will note that some of the facts that need to be established at trial are within the realm of expert testimony and not something to which a lay witness is qualified to attest.

Taking those facts, they then work back to considering what kind of person or profession knows and can explain those facts. Once they have an idea of those general parameters, they will then run a series of searches designed to find potential candidates.

For example, after educating themselves on the subject, they might explore faculty departments at universities teaching the subject, people writing books in the subject, and individuals working in the particular industry.

There are also firms with experts in various subjects on call that can help with this process. They will work with the lawyer to understand what kind of expertise is required and help them find individuals within their network that may have that expertise. Other firms have a stable of testifying experts who can be contacted directly.

Some experts, like damages experts and forensics experts, work as a testifying expert all the time. Their expertise is needed in litigation commonly enough that this can be a huge part, or all, of their business.

Other times, the discipline or technology that requires expert testimony in a case is very specialized and peculiar to that case. In those situations, the lawyer may have to rely more on their own careful, individualized research to find someone appropriate for that role.

Smart Trial Lawyers Are Careful to Hire Smart, Principled Expert Witnesses

It is important for a lawyer to ensure that they find a true expert in the subject. If they cannot find an expert in that precise subject, they must ensure the expert's expertise has a logical, close, and very reasonable tie to the area in which the expert will testify.

It is important to carefully match the right expert to the right subject because the more direct expertise the expert has, the more weight their opinion has. The jury is entitled to give the opinion as much or as little weight as it deems appropriate.

The jury and judge must be satisfied that the lawyer's chosen expert truly has the expertise or experience to provide the testimony being presented by that person. If not, it is either worthless or worse—it makes the party look dishonest for using them.

Since the expert will likely serve as the lawyer's teacher during the case, the lawyer will want to procure a true expert. Sometimes non-testifying consultants also fill this role. The expert can be the lawyer's guide to the technology or discipline at issue in the case, and they are relying on the expert's breadth and depth of knowledge to master the basic issues.

They will also count on the expert to help them detect flaws in the opposing expert's presentation and opportunities for their case that might not be readily apparent.

Now, in response, the opposing party may hire a true expert to oppose the chosen expert. One may feel outgunned by some flashy expert appearing on the other side. But a meritorious, well-grounded, persuasive expert opinion will beat a flashy but insipid expert every time. Or the opponent will hire someone who is really not an expert, a hack who will say whatever they want.

Either way, a real expert will be needed to help the jury cut through these distractions and understand why such tactics are misleading, not probative, and should not be trusted.

Parties Should Thoroughly Vet Their Experts

Solid expertise is not the only thing to look for.

Professionalism in an expert witness is also an absolute must. An expert witness represents a huge outlay of resources for the client and creates a certain amount of risk in a case that a lawyer cannot totally control.

> Failure to properly vet an expert can create unpleasant surprises later. Trial counsel and client should assume that the opponent is highly motivated to find any and all dirt on one's expert to either show they are sloppy, are an expert in something else, made a mistake, are biased, are paid off, or anything else that will undercut the strength of their testimony.

For example, in federal court, the expert must prepare a fulsome report on their opinion, and while the lawyers can help, it is still important to employ a professional, natural self-starter who accepts personal responsibility for doing well in their role.

Also, even though the expert is providing an unbiased report based on the facts and analysis, the jury will still associate the expert with the party presenting them. So their presentation should be well organized, well supported, and otherwise inspire confidence in its correctness.

Honesty and a good rapport are both super important. The expert has to feel comfortable and confident enough to convey to the lawyer any concerns and questions and obtain or receive all the information they need to render an honest opinion.

That is their job: to present an honest opinion on the subject, not to "help" the client by stretching the facts or the analysis in their favor. It is the strength of the expert's opinion, based on the true merits of the case, that is probative. If the merits are not so good, then the client should find that out as early as possible.

Moreover, the lawyer should not be shy about thoroughly reviewing the expert's professional and personal background; the expert's past statements in all their past publications, expert reports, deposition, and trial transcripts, etc.; and their licenses and certifications. The lawyer should also call their references. A lawyer should know about any previous *Daubert* challenges and the grounds for, and outcome of, those challenges.

> **Daubert challenge** refers to a motion challenging the admissibility of the expert's planned testimony.
>
> If an expert did not survive a *Daubert* challenge in previous cases, that is important information to know before using them in one's case. It may be that their testimony is better suited in the present case, but there should be no surprises after a party has disclosed their expert to the opponent.

This expert will be a representation of your client to the jury. So they must have impeccable credentials and appear to be honest, reasonable, and professional.

Ideally, the lawyer should seek someone with testifying skills and experience. Not everyone is cut out for delivering testimony. Someone who generally understands the process and can listen to the question and formulate appropriate answers is a plus.

Not that a really green expert is a deal breaker. Some experts have actually learned bad habits with other lawyers, so in some situations, it might be better to work with a clean slate.

For all these reasons, it is critical to have a robust selection process up front and to find an expert with all the qualities needed to put on quality expert testimony.

Expert Disclosures

In some courts, including federal court, expert reports are a required disclosure in a case.

Expert Reports Are Intended to Provide All the Information Necessary to Challenge the Opinion

Using the federal courts as an example, an expert report is intended to be a full disclosure of the expert's opinions. According to Federal Rule of Civil Procedure 26(a)(2)(B), expert reports must include:

i.   A complete statement of all opinions the witness will express and the basis and reasons for them;

ii. The facts or data considered by the witness in forming them;

iii. Any exhibits that will be used to summarize or support them;

iv. The witness' qualifications, including a list of all publications authored in the previous 10 years;

v.   A list of all other cases in which, during the previous 4 years, the witness testified as an expert at trial or by deposition; and

vi.   A statement of the compensation to be paid for the study and testimony in the case.

> Expert reports in federal court should fully disclose the expert's opinion and the bases and reasons for it to the opponent and its expert.
>
> The receiving party's expert will then provide a rebuttal report, and in some but not all cases, the first expert will provide a reply to the rebuttal report.

The court will often set deadlines in the case for opening expert disclosures, rebuttal disclosures, and any reply disclosures if the parties want them and the court grants them. Often the court will set a deadline for when the experts need to be deposed and when the parties must initiate any Daubert challenges.

The federal rules were very deliberate in determining what needs to be in an expert report, and an opponent can seek to exclude the expert testimony if the report is less than forthcoming about all the required information.

Subsections (iv) through (vi) are easy to comply with, whereas subsections (i) through (iii) are trickier but extremely important.

Lawyers must work closely with inexperienced experts to ensure they are meeting subsections (i) through (iii). Any opinions not disclosed in the report(s) or in the expert's deposition will not be permitted at trial. Further, the entire basis for the opinion—what facts they reviewed, what analyses they applied, what assumptions they made, and what they were based on—must be fully disclosed in the report or, on the margin, in the expert's deposition.

Summarizing exhibits must be included as well, although that is often part of complying with (i) and (ii) because experts often use such exhibits to help fully explain the bases and reasons for their opinion. The report also has to be signed by the expert, and all the opinions in it must be those of the expert.

The expert report is a disclosure to the opponent and its expert and is not filed with the court. The disclosure is intended so the opponent's expert, after reviewing it, can understand it completely. The opponent's expert can also prepare a responsive opinion including an explanation of why the first expert analysis is flawed.

The opposing lawyer can also use it to prepare for the expert's deposition where they can learn more about the analyses conducted. They can then prepare a rebuttal opinion with their own expert and/or prepare for cross-examination of this expert at trial.

The Expert Should Be Prepared for Depositions

Expert depositions are an important part of this process. The expert must defend their opinion against the questioning of the opposing lawyer and document the errors and/or improper analysis by the opposing expert.

The deposition is an opportunity to probe the expert's professional and sometimes personal background; clear up any ambiguities in the report or exhibits; question their assumptions; and pose hypothetical and other questions to test the robustness of their analysis.

In federal court, what is said in deposition can augment the report such that the scope of the expert's ultimate opinion at trial may be somewhat broader after the deposition.

As with any witness, good witness prep is essential. Many experts think they are better testifiers than they are and underestimate the challenges that an aggressive and highly motivated opposing counsel may present.

Also, significant time may pass between the time the expert wrote their report and the deposition. The lawyer and their team should take time to review this report and the expert's bases and reasons for the report. The lawyer and expert should discuss any possible weaknesses in the analysis and how those issues should be addressed.

"Daubert" and "Frye": Preventing Junk Science from Entering the Courtroom

U.S. courts primarily use a variation of either the "Daubert" or "Frye" standard when assessing the admissibility of an expert's potential testimony. If the court concludes, using these standards, that the expert would be putting, in effect, "junk science" in front of the jury, they will declare the testimony inadmissible and exclude the expert entirely. In some cases, the judge may limit the opinions the expert can give.

The basic standard for expert testimony outlined in the federal rules is that it provides scientific knowledge that will assist the trier of fact to understand or determine a fact in issue.

Frye Requires a Generally Accepted Test

The *Frye* standard is named after a 1923 case called *Frye v. United States*, 293 F. 1013 (D.C. Cir. 1923). That case holds an expert opinion is admissible if the basis for the scientific technique is generally accepted as reliable by the relevant scientific community.

This can be a difficult showing to get a fix on. In every field, there is a gray area in which a new theory or scientific technique moves toward general acceptance, whatever that is. It is often difficult to determine just when it has become "generally accepted" by the field as a whole.

As technologies and the world become more sophisticated, that determination becomes even trickier.

Daubert Is More Generous Toward Admissibility

In 1993, the Supreme Court overruled *Frye* for use in federal cases as inconsistent with the liberal view of evidence encouraged by the Federal Rules of Civil Procedure. It announced a new, more flexible standard in *Daubert v. Merrell Dow Pharmaceuticals, Inc.*, 509 U.S. 579 (1993).

Instead of trying to measure admissibility using the "general acceptance" test, the *Daubert* case spoke of the court having a "gatekeeping responsibility" and outlined a framework focused on relevance and reliability.

The Court emphasized the overall flexibility of the analysis. It then set out a list of non-exclusive factors to determine whether the testimony meets the federal rules:

- Whether a theory or technique can be, and has been, tested. The court distinguished scientific analysis from other forms of analysis by noting that it uses testable and tested hypotheses.

- Whether the theory or technique has been subject to peer review and publication. While the court noted that publication does not ensure reliability, exposure to the scientific community suggests the technique has withstood a certain amount of rigor.

- Whether there was a known or potential rate of error of a "particular scientific technique."

- Whether standards exist to control the technique's operation and whether those standards have been maintained.

- Whether the proponent can identify a relevant scientific community and show some degree of acceptance within that community (like *Frye*).

The Court also stressed the use of vigorous cross-examination to ensure that the opinion of the experts is given a proper amount of weight.

Six years later, the Court held in *Kumho Tire Co. v. Carmichael*, 526 U.S 137 (1999) that the same standard used in the *Daubert* case should be used for non-scientific testimony, for example, for technical or other specialized knowledge.

As a result, today all the federal courts and the great majority of U.S. states employ some variety of the *Daubert* standard. Notably some of the most populous states, including California, Illinois, and New York, still use some form of *Frye*. Florida just switched from *Frye* to *Daubert* in mid-2019.

The *Daubert* decision created more flexibility in admitting expert testimony by including a multi-factor test and relying on the court as a gatekeeper rather than relying on the relevant scientific community.

The *Daubert* case thus broadened the list of factors to be considered and introduced more flexibility into the process. In addition, the *Daubert* test relies heavily on the court's gatekeeping role rather than on the relevant scientific community.

Whether this is a good thing depends on the nature of the scientific, technical, or other specialized testimony to be presented in a case. In some cases, a party does not want that flexibility. For an easy example, in a criminal case, the defendant might want the parties to employ more rigor to the test through the *Frye* test, hoping the government's expert might not qualify to give testimony.

Daubert Challenges

Striking or limiting the testimony of an expert can leave a gap in the opponent's case, so it is wise for a lawyer to at least consider whether such a challenge is a possibility.

The lawyer can challenge an expert's testimony based on *Daubert* at pretty much any time, subject to two limitations. One is any deadline the court has set for the timing of such motions.

> There are multiple opportunities to challenge an expert on the basis of *Daubert*.

The other limitation is getting too close to the trial. At some point, the court may view it as being unduly prejudicial to eliminate one party's expert witness. Nonetheless, bringing the challenge too early may permit the opponent time to cure the problems identified by way of an amended report.

A *Daubert* challenge focuses on the admissibility of the expert's opinion, and thus is limited to challenging the expert's competence and the relevance and reliability of their opinion. Put another way, it focuses on the reliability of the process rather than the conclusion or result of the opinion.

The burden of proof on a *Daubert* motion is on the defending party to show that the testimony is, in fact, admissible—specifically that the expert is qualified and that the testimony is relevant and reliable for its purpose.

Daubert challenges may be brought by formal *Daubert*-based motion or in connection with a summary judgment motion. *Daubert* can also be the subject of a motion *in limine* (discussed in chapter nine), or as an objection when the expert gives their testimony. The parties have an opportunity to re-raise the issue in the post-trial briefing as well.

Challenges might include a full evidentiary hearing. That question depends largely on the judge's preferences and the procedural posture of the challenge. An evidentiary hearing may give the defending expert a chance to provide an explanation of their testimony, which may not be preferred by the movant.

The defending party should keep *Daubert* in mind when selecting its expert and helping them prepare their opinions. It can ultimately meet its burden of proof by explaining why the methodology they are using is reliable and showing published articles and other third-party statements that support the reliability of the methodology.

Having all this information thought out ahead of time and ready to go when the challenge comes is optimal.

Other Attacks on the Expert

Daubert is not the only way one can dismantle an expert. A well-planned cross-examination can be devastating.

Weak Attacks on Most Expert Witnesses

One fairly obvious kind of attack is on some bias that the expert had in preparing their analysis in the case. Since experts are paid, the opponent may suggest that the expert's testimony has been influenced by their fee. However, usually both sides have an expert, and most jurors understand that experts do this for a living and must be paid. So this is not usually a persuasive attack.

There may be other biases at play, however. For example, if the expert always represents defendants, that might be a point to pursue where they are again representing a defendant. The problem with bias-based attacks is that they can be weak on support. This makes the lawyer sound like a bully, especially with a sympathetic expert witness.

Another attack is that the lawyers really prepared the report. The reality, though, is that lawyers may legitimately assist in preparation. We want them to. It ensures the lawyers have given careful thought and applied their own critical skills along the way. This assists the expert in preparing a strong, robust analysis that is actually helpful to the jury and that can withstand attack from the opponent.

That said, it is important for the expert to "own" everything that is in the report. So even if a section was drafted by a lawyer, the expert must accept every word of it as their own or modify it until it is their own.

Better Attacks on Expert Witnesses

Stronger attacks on the expert target the merits, and there are three general areas to attack. The first area is the factual investigation and review that the expert did in connection with their analysis:

- Did the expert ask for and receive all the materials they should have in order to perform the analysis that they did?

- Are there other documents or evidence or facts they should have but did not review or consider in performing the analysis?

- Would their opinion have been different if they did consider those facts?

- What did they base their assumptions on, and were they sensible assumptions?

- If those assumptions turn out to be wrong, does that invalidate their opinion?

Litigation teams hiring an expert should carefully vet that expert to avoid any attack on the expert's past work and should work with them to ensure they have a robust and well-supported analysis for their opinion in the case.

The second area is to attack the expert's methodology. If it is not widely accepted, or not widely accepted for use the way they are using it, then that might be an avenue for attack:

- What are the best practices of a scientist utilizing this methodology?

- Did the expert use them?

- Did they change something in how they practiced the methodology that yielded a different conclusion?

- Had they used best practices, would this have yielded the same result?

The third area is attacking the expert's conclusion:

- Is the conclusion that the expert drew a sensible one given the facts, the investigation, and the methodology employed?

- If it is a scientific conclusion, is it reproducible?

- Have other scientists in that field reached similar conclusions on similar facts? If it is not a scientifically-based conclusion but instead something based, for example, on their general experience or knowledge, that fuzziness may be something to attack.

- What was their reasoning?

- What analysis did they use?

- Have others ever used that analysis?

- What would be the result if different facts were applied?

If the expert is on shaky ground to start with, they will have trouble pointing to the support for their conclusion. This will undercut it in front of the jury.

Expert Management

Experts are people too and require a certain amount of care and feeding along the way. Good experts really care about what position they are taking. They care that it is a strong, defensible one at the end of the day. Their name and reputation are on the line, after all.

Ensuring the expert has a strong defensible opinion that will withstand the rigors of *Daubert* and cross-examination requires lawyer support for that expert throughout that process. The lawyer supports the expert by:

- ensuring the expert actually has the appropriate expertise

- understanding their opinion and analysis and methodology

- ensuring that they have all the materials they need to do a careful and thorough investigation and arrive at a robust conclusion

- pointing the expert to key facts that are possibly relevant within the sometimes hundreds of thousands or millions of documents in the case and helping them find other facts that they recognize are relevant

- asking smart questions that challenge the expert's analysis

- editing the expert report for clarity

- "black hatting" them at deposition prep

- looking after them when defending their deposition, making sure they do not get too tired and do not create sloppy testimony.

Litigators play an important role in ensuring the success of an expert presentation. A smart litigator must anticipate all attacks on an expert and foil them.

Experts very often have a limited view into the case as a whole. They may then feel concerned that they are overextended, meaning their opinion might be undercut somehow by facts the lawyer didn't share with them.

Anticipating those concerns and addressing them up front can ensure that the expert is not distracted by some concern that does not matter. A good rapport with the expert is helpful in identifying and quickly addressing these concerns.

CHAPTER NINE

PRETRIAL PREPARATION ACTIVITIES

So at this point, the case has made it through motions to dismiss, documentary discovery, depositions, expert discovery, and dispositive motion practice, and it is time to put it all together and prepare for the trial.

Using its framework of evidence and good judgment, the team will ensure there are no gaps in the evidence as trial approaches. It will have conceived of, and developed, its trial themes along the way.

The executive or in-house counsel needs to understand what materials are being prepared so as to be in a better position to participate and supervise in the team's preparation.

So here I demystify the pretrial process, which reduces stress and makes for more robust decisions along the way.

<u>Steps Taken Earlier Provide the Materials Needed for Pretrial Preparation</u>

A trial lawyer will have prepared for trial from the first day they got the case.

As they are talking to the client and learning the facts, they may start thinking about the themes of the case: Is this a David vs Goliath story? Is this a story about greed? Usually multiple themes could be developed from the basic facts.

> **Trial themes** should be considered and developed from the beginning of the case. The framework of evidence is designed to guide the litigation team's decisions throughout the case and to ensure that the themes and story come together for trial.

The framework of evidence prepared early on in the case should not have been forgotten along the way. As the parties have obtained the facts to fill in the required elements of their claims and defenses from the documentary evidence and depositions, the framework should have been filled in.

Also, by this time the parties may have obtained some admissions from the opponent that have resolved some parts of the framework.

Depositions have been taken and the documents received have been analyzed and the key materials identified. All the pieces are there, and the puzzle just needs to be assembled.

Pretrial Conference

In the case schedule, there is usually a date set for a final pretrial conference. At this conference, the parties will discuss with the judge how they think the trial will go.

The parties are often asked to work together to draft a pretrial conference order in advance that summarizes the information the judge needs to decide how the trial will proceed.

For example, on the website for the Central District of California, there is a template for a proposed final pretrial conference order. In it, the parties are expected to address these topics:

- Parties and Pleadings: This is an opportunity to remind the court if claims or defenses appearing in the pleadings have been resolved, or if any of the parties have settled along the way.

- Jurisdiction: A simple statement about jurisdiction and venue can be inserted.

- Trial Duration: The parties must fill in their estimate of trial time (or estimates, if they do not agree).

- Jury Trial: The parties can affirm that they are having a jury trial and tell the court when they will submit their "Agreed

Upon Set of Jury Instructions and Verdict Forms" and the "Joint Statement re Disputed Instructions, Verdicts, etc." to the court.

- Admitted Facts: The parties insert the facts that are admitted and therefore need not be proven.

- Stipulated Facts: The parties insert the facts that are stipulated to between the parties but can still be subject to objection at the trial.

- Parties' Claims and Defenses: The parties insert the claims and defenses and the elements of each claim and defense.

- Remaining Triable Issues: Having set forth the elements of each claim and defense and identified the list of admitted facts, this leaves the parties with the set of issues that must be tried.

- Discovery: Often there is some outstanding discovery dispute or issue that needs to still be resolved. That can be identified here. Otherwise, the parties may just tell the court that discovery has been completed.

- Disclosures and Exhibit List: The federal rules include required pretrial disclosures that the parties must make to each other about a month before trial. This includes the names and contact information for witnesses they plan to present, either live or by deposition, and an identification of the documents and exhibits they plan to use. In this section of the draft order, the parties will note that the disclosures have been made, or not, and will reference the exhibit list, which they have attached to the draft.

- Witness Lists. The parties must list the witnesses they plan to call other than solely for impeachment, meaning to call out the dishonesty of another witness. Sometimes the court requires the witnesses to be placed in "will call" and "may call" subcategories.

- Motions *in Limine* (discussed in more detail below). This section will suggest a date by which the motions *in limine* will be filed with the court, if one is not already set. It will also apprise the court of what motions *in limine* are planned. The court will expect the parties to have already met and conferred about those motions, but it is a good idea nonetheless to tell the court that it has been done.

- Bifurcation: The trial can be divided into phases. All the evidence can be presented about one set of issues first, and the evidence about another set of issues can be presented in a new phase. One natural split may be between the presentation of liability and damages, for example. This is where the parties explain their respective plans or joint plan for bifurcation.

- Admissions: The parties list here all the admissions that have been made.

The court can then enter this document as an order with or without modifications, and it becomes part of the trial record.

As you can see, many time-intensive pretrial activities have already taken place by the time the parties prepare the proposed final pretrial conference order.

Exhibit Lists and Exhibits

The whole point of pretrial disclosures, like discovery, is to avoid disruptive surprises along the way.

The parties should start the trial with roughly the same information available to them, giving them a full opportunity to test, challenge, or rebut that information on the merits.

Accordingly, the exhibit list should include all the exhibits the parties believe they will be presenting at trial. When the parties can agree on the presentation of certain exhibits—for example, the contract that the parties are suing each other over—that is a "joint exhibit" and will be identified as such on the list. The parties' other exhibits are identified as plaintiff's and defendant's exhibits.

All the exhibits must be numbered in advance and stamped with that number. A common convention is to use PX, DX, and JX to denote the plaintiff's, defendant's, and any joint exhibits. The exhibits will be identified by these numbers throughout the trial.

The exhibits will then be printed out and placed in binders with tabs for easy access. Each party and the court gets a full set of PX, DX, and JX exhibits, and the exhibits are also put in binders for the witness to have on the stand.

In a large business trial, with many different claims and defenses being tried, there can be literally thousands of potential exhibits on the list. While this may be a fulsome disclosure because it fairly includes everything the party anticipates using, the sheer volume of the exhibits may obscure what is actually intended for the presentation.

> Not only does the trial team have to identify the exhibits needed for trial, but it also must be aware of whether those exhibits are admissible, and if not, take steps to establish those facts some other way.

Sometimes the court will limit the number of exhibits each party may put on the list to force the parties to be more selective at an earlier stage in the process. Realistically, there is no chance that the parties will have time to present every exhibit on their list.

Also, the court can require parties to notify each other of which specific exhibits will be used with a witness a day or two before the witness is put on the stand.

Objections Must Be Asserted and Resolved

All the non-stipulated evidence planned for the trial is subject to objection by the other side. The exhibit list, therefore, will usually include the objections asserted as to each exhibit and sometimes a response to those objections.

Having this information well before the trial begins makes it easier for the parties to figure out how they will deal with those objections. Failure to identify the objections in advance may result in them being waived.

Objections may be dealt with in the course of the trial, but this can be disruptive and distracting for the jurors. Also, the parties benefit from knowing the court's answer to some of these objections earlier rather than later.

Accordingly, the court may require the parties to identify and brief some number of "high-priority objections" before the trial starts. Some courts do not like to rule on objections on the fly and will permit the resolution of some "high-priority objections" before every court day.

Back at the Ranch

In addition to all the planned exhibits, trying a business case also means having all the other documents produced in discovery, or at least some logical portion of them, fully searchable. A skilled team should be back at the office running those searches instantaneously.

This permits a trial team to quickly find impeachment evidence and explore information that emerges at trial. A trial team without this capability will be at a disadvantage.

> **Impeachment**—not the presidential kind—refers to the process of calling into question the credibility of an individual testifying in a trial.
>
> For example, let's say at trial the witness claims that they were disappointed by the poor quality of the opposing party's products from the very beginning of the relationship.
>
> This witness' testimony would be impeached by emails they wrote at the time praising the high quality of the opposing party's products.

The team may also consider creating blow-ups of the key exhibits. While there will be technology in the courtroom to display certain materials to the jury, having a physical blow-up can be helpful because it can be displayed throughout an entire witness presentation. It need not be taken down every time you want to show something else.

Witness List

The witness list should include all the witnesses that each party plans to put on at trial, again erring on the side of inclusiveness. Usually this list will be divided between will-calls and may-calls. Witnesses not on the list will likely not be permitted to testify, other than for impeachment.

At the beginning of a jury trial, the court will often ask the jurors if they know any of the witnesses or lawyers. The court wants to determine if they have a connection that might make them biased for or against a party. The witness list is often used for this and should be prepared with that purpose in mind as well.

Determining who belongs on the witness list to begin with is not necessarily an easy task, particularly in a large trial. The parties must present their case primarily through witnesses and documents, and the documents may only come into evidence (absent stipulation) through the testimony of the witnesses. So the planned witnesses should have the knowledge necessary to establish all the facts needed to prove one's claims or defenses.

Sometimes more than one witness may have such information, so the team will need to decide which witness should be used.

In deciding this, the team should take into account the individuality of the witnesses, as some may have various qualities and histories that may be less than ideal at trial. For example, some people just do not look credible. Jurors look closely at each witness and use everything they've learned in their time on Earth to determine whether they should believe this person on the stand.

What someone actually says is only part of the story. The nonverbal cues they give off can be just as, or even more, important. Trial lawyers must be sensitive to how their witnesses are likely to appear on the stand.

> **Carrying the water** refers to a witness' ability to testify credibly and appropriately on certain subjects. Trial lawyers might say they are unsure a particular expert should try to carry the water on some point and consider presenting that information through a percipient witness.

Witnesses also come with their own personal history and sometimes even case-relevant baggage. Sometimes while working up the case, the lawyer learns of events that a witness experienced that are unhelpful to the theme of the case and that did not come out at the deposition stage.

There is likely an explanation for whatever happened. But it is easier to avoid using that witness because even with the explanation, it might create a huge distraction for the jury at best.

Witness Outlines

For each friendly witness, the lawyer should prepare an outline of the examination. It should include:

- the objectives to be met through that witness' testimony

- the questions to be asked of that witness

- the exhibits that will be introduced through or used with that witness

- the anticipated cross-examination of that witness

- potential avenues for rebuttal

For each hostile witness, a cross-examination outline must be prepared, based on the anticipated direct.

The trial outlines will be modified as the trial progresses, but they need to be prepared well in advance. There will be no time to write them as the case gets close to trial. Plus, this is a good way of knowing how the trial should unfold. The sooner the lawyer has them, the sooner they can see gaps and opportunities that should be addressed.

Expert witness outlines also need to be drafted. Presenting an expert's testimony requires careful planning to ensure that the testimony is well supported and understandable, and the expert is otherwise credible.

The jury may be aided by creating demonstratives, such as PowerPoint slides, that the expert can use to walk the jurors through the facts and analysis that they used to arrive at their conclusions.

Witness files also need to be prepared. The parties will prepare a file for each planned witness that includes:

- the witness' deposition transcript (if any), and any summary thereof

- the direct and cross-examination outlines for that witness

- the exhibits to be presented through that witness and of which the witness has knowledge

For an expert, the file will also include:

- their expert reports

- any rebuttal reports

- the materials the expert used for their analysis

- materials on the expert's background, including any curriculum vitae and any past writings, deposition, and trial transcripts.

This witness file is used by the lawyers to prepare for the witness' preparation and examination.

Witness Subpoenas

Some of the witnesses in a business trial are the client's employees or representatives, or are otherwise "friendly." They require just a heads-up as to when they are to be prepared and when and where they will appear in court.

Other witnesses will not show up unless they are compelled to, and that is what trial subpoenas are for.

However, there are limitations on the reach of trial subpoenas, even for witnesses affiliated with a party to the case. If a necessary but unfriendly witness is outside the territory of the subpoena power and the opponent does not agree to make that witness available at trial, the witness' testimony may have to be presented by deposition.

Deposition Designations

For various reasons, deposition testimony may need to be presented at trial. Even for witnesses that will likely appear, deposition testimony must be prepared because a witness could become unavailable.

Accordingly, the court requires the preparation and exchange of **deposition designations** by the parties' lawyers. These designations indicate what portions of the testimony the respective sides plan to play in their case-in-chief (their primary case, not rebuttal case).

Where one party has designated a portion of the transcript, the other party may make "counter-designations" of testimony, which complete or explain what was conveyed in the initial designation. The other party can also make their own affirmative designations that are subject to counter-designation.

Like witness lists and exhibit lists, designations are over-inclusive. The parties always try to preserve the ability to use whatever they might need for the trial.

The parties preparing the designations must work together in earnest to try to resolve as many objections as they can or incur the wrath of the trial court.

Whatever objections remain must be resolved somehow. This will likely be the subject of pretrial briefing, or it could be resolved for each witness a couple days before the witness' testimony is to be played.

When the objections have been resolved, then the video deposition testimony is cut down to just the portions that will be played, and transcripts are prepared for those portions.

Very often in a large trial, the designations will be negotiated down over time, so several iterations of each video have to be prepared along the way.

Besides the designations, all the depositions taken in the case must be organized, available, and searchable during the trial.

Pretrial Pleadings and Discovery

The pleadings, other key filings and orders, and the written discovery record must be organized and readily available at trial.

What is in the pleadings shapes the scope of the trial. Pleadings also contain admissions by the parties.

Admissions are an extremely powerful form of evidence for two reasons.

- They are **non-hearsay**, which makes them easy to admit as evidence.

- They are hard to walk away from.

  - Judicial admissions may not be controverted with other evidence, and the party making them is stuck with them.

  - Lesser admissions are great impeachment evidence.

Motions and rulings throughout the case also affect the scope of the trial. They often contain party admissions and provide ammunition for the parties regarding the judge's views throughout the case.

There are many other uses for these items, but suffice it to say, it is critical to have this information readily available. In complex cases, there may need to be indices—and ideally, the ability to search electronically—so helpful information may be found almost instantaneously.

Interrogatories, requests for admission, and requests for production, along with their respective responses and every iteration thereof, must be organized and readily available and searchable at trial as well.

The responses to discovery may be the subject of witness impeachment, or they may be presented as affirmative evidence. Responses to requests for interrogatories—and especially to requests for admission—can be great fun at trial to demonstrate the ridiculously unreasonable pretrial attitude of the opponent, the resistance to admitting basic truths, and the like.

Indeed, written discovery should be crafted in the first instance with the trial presentation in mind.

Motions *in Limine*

Before the trial occurs, the parties may file one or more **motions *in limine***, which are short motions seeking to exclude particular types of evidence from being presented at the trial.

Parties should be creative about motions *in limine* because they shape what is presented at the trial. For example, a party may seek to exclude evidence relating to the outcomes of similar cases to avoid prejudicing the jury. A party litigating against a popular public figure might want to limit the presentation of unrelated evidence about all the charity work they do because it generates sympathy and distracts from a fair review of the facts in the case.

> By maintaining a list of defensive and offensive **motions *in limine*** through the pre-trial phases of the case, trial counsel stays focused on what is or is not coming into evidence at trial.

Motions *in limine* are usually based on one or more of the evidentiary rules in the jurisdiction.

Like other motions in the case, the opponent can oppose. The court will usually resolve these motions before trial but may hold over the decision on some of them to see how the trial unfolds a little before ruling. The judge has more context at that point.

Pocket Briefs

Motions *in limine* are often limited in number by the judge. There are also usually certain evidentiary or other disputes that are anticipated to come up at the trial but may not come up until the middle of trial or may not come up at all.

Or they are likely to come up, but the lawyer judges it to be more advantageous if the dispute is taken up by the court later. The judge may want the benefit of the additional context provided by the witnesses and evidence presented by that later point.

Such issues are good candidates for a pocket brief, which is a short draft motion that the lawyer drafts but holds in their "pocket." They can pull it out at any time, spruce it up, and file it with the court for a swift resolution.

Besides the motions *in limine*, a member of the trial team will prepare pocket briefs on key issues in advance. They will also stay on the lookout for additional issues that may require mid-case briefing.

Neutral Statement of the Case

At the beginning of the trial, the judge will often give a short and neutral introduction to the case to the jurors. This statement is a paragraph or two and tells the jurors what the case is about at a high level, outlining the basic contentions of the parties.

As with many pretrial submissions, the parties should try to submit a jointly agreed statement for the court to read. But if this is impossible, the court may use the competing submissions of the parties to arrive at its own neutral statement.

Voir Dire

Voir dire refers to the examination of the jurors by the lawyers and/or judge that takes place during the process of jury selection.

The jurors are where the rubber meets the road at trial since they are going to "find the facts," meaning decide on what the ultimate facts are.

Voir dire is one of the rare times the trial lawyers will have direct contact with the jurors, as opposed to presenting to them.

It will also be the only time the trial lawyers can solicit information from the jurors, at least before the trial is over.

The primary goal of this selection process is to ensure the court seats a fair and impartial panel of jurors, but voir dire has other purposes as well, and a skilled attorney will craft the voir dire examination with all these purposes in mind.

One purpose is to gather information about the jurors that will help the lawyers consider how the jurors are likely to view and decide on their case.

Another is to determine how influential each juror is likely to be within the group of people that are going to sit on the jury.

In business trials, the lawyers will have carefully considered the themes of the case. They will also have an idea of the types of values and attitudes that people hold that make those themes resonate, either for or against their cause.

So another purpose of voir dire is to ascertain who might have values or attitudes sympathetic to or hostile to the lawyer's case.

In jurisdictions where the rules require unanimity among the jurors, one persuasive juror that is hostile to the lawyer's client or case could do a great deal of damage by unfairly swaying the other jurors against that party.

> Trial lawyers use voir dire to subtly lay groundwork for the party's position.

The other purposes of voir dire are to provide some background and context for the case to the jurors and to develop a positive rapport with them if possible. The lawyer's questions will be crafted so they highlight certain issues within the case, allowing the lawyer to see the jurors' reaction to the presentation they will see in the case, and determine their likely attitudes toward those issues.

In doing this, the lawyer usually has an opportunity to lay some groundwork for the party's position during the questioning as they probe the juror for the juror's opinions.

Voir dire involves asking questions about the individual jurors' personal background, experience, values, opinions, and beliefs. Importantly, it involves doing so in front of the other jurors.

It is important to be respectful of the jurors and converse with them, encouraging them to participate honestly and openly. For example, in a case where a company has sued someone for taking its alleged trade secrets after leaving the company, the defendant's attorney might ask the jurors if they've ever taken anything upon leaving a job before, and whether they think it is acceptable to take certain types of information as opposed to other types, and what types of information they believe are proprietary and confidential to a company, and what types of information they do not. Then the lawyer may probe the subject with the jurors who answered that they had that experience.

An important part of the process is actively listening to what each juror is saying and using the responses to generate follow-up questions to that and the other jurors in a natural way. When the jurors appreciate that they are being listened to and understood, that can have a positive impact on their willingness to participate.

Also, when the questioner acknowledges that having biases is part of being human, this makes it easier for the juror to be honest about acknowledging their own biases.

The questioner invites discussion by using open-ended questions, like "what are your views on . . ." and encourages candor by not using judgment-laden language that may make jurors feel self-conscious in front of the other jurors if they don't answer the question in a particular way.

While all of this is going on, the questioning lawyer, as well as the other lawyers in the room, is listening to the jurors' responses and watching their nonverbal cues, noting down the responses and trying to get a sense of whether the jurors are leaders or followers within a group.

At the same time, the lawyer may have a team running internet searches to gather whatever information can be learned about the jurors to advise the questioner in real time or to analyze later. Social media is a treasure trove of personal information that can show lawyers the values and belief systems that the jurors hold. Some jurisdictions have restrictions on this kind of activity, however.

A jury consultant may also be present. They will have analyzed the case and helped the lawyers figure out which types of jurors might be beneficial or harmful to their cause. The consultant will help the lawyers become familiar with the jury pool where the case is to be tried, help develop themes for the case that are likely to resonate with the jurors, and prepare voir dire questions for the lawyers to ask.

Jury Instructions

Another pretrial project for both parties is preparing and negotiating a set of jury instructions. The jury instructions are the legal rules that will be read and provided in writing to the jurors at the end of the trial presentation and before they go into the jury room to deliberate.

At this point, the jurors will have seen evidence presented by both sides and will discuss that evidence and try to resolve discrepancies in that evidence to "find" the actual facts. The jurors must then apply the facts to the legal rules provided in order to determine a verdict.

Some jury instructions explain the basic process to the jury. These instructions are an overview that explains what they've heard, what parts of it they are to consider and what parts they cannot, and how they will apply the jury instructions, etc.

Other very basic instructions explain how to be a responsible juror, for example, telling them they are not to talk with each other or others about the case outside the jury room until a verdict has been reached. Or advising them that they should not be using social media or other sources to gather facts from outside the case.

The language used in these basic instructions is usually fairly uncontroversial and can be readily stipulated to.

The bulk of the jury instructions are substantive in nature. They outline the elements of the claims and defenses in the case for the jury so they can at some point match the facts they've found to those elements. The judge must decide the law that will apply to the case.

There are sample and "model" jury instructions available as a starting point in most jurisdictions. However, applying the claims and defenses must be guided to some extent by precedential case law and other authorities.

The lawyers on each side will want to create a tailor-made set of proposed jury instructions that are appropriate given the facts presented by their case. Each party's take on what the facts are will also likely influence the decision as to what language that party will propose in its jury instructions.

> The **burden of proof** refers to the plaintiff's obligation to prove entitlement to the relief sought.
>
> If the plaintiff meets that burden, then the burden of proof shifts to the defendant to establish that a defense applies and/or to prove entitlement based on a counterclaim.

An important part of the jury instructions is helping the jurors understand who has the burden of proof on a certain claim or defense, and what level of proof is required. If there is a dispute as to which party has the burden of proof on a particular issue, that question may have to be briefed by the parties so the court can determine it.

Once the parties have each completed a set of jury instructions, they must meet and confer to negotiate over any differences between the two sets. The parties will discuss the reasons for their respective proposals, the supporting case law for example, and make compromises.

The **standard of proof** refers to how certain the fact finder needs to be about the evidence to establish proof.

In a civil matter, the usual standard of proof is the **preponderance of the evidence**, which can be thought of as just a little more than 50 percent.

Some questions in civil cases have the higher standard of **clear and convincing evidence**.

The **beyond a reasonable doubt** standard is a standard used in criminal cases.

Any jury instructions that remain in dispute after that process will be presented to the judge for decision. This process can continue throughout the presentation of evidence and may be wrapped up relatively close to when the jurors need to start their deliberations.

Verdict Forms

The verdict form steers the jurors through the decisions they must make to apply the law to the facts and determine the outcome of the claims and defenses.

Verdict forms vary in their level of specificity. Very often the plaintiff believes short and sweet is to its advantage, while the defendant would rather force the jurors to jump through a bunch of hoops along the way, making it tougher to find in favor of the plaintiff.

Accordingly, the verdict form usually has to be negotiated along with the jury instructions.

The verdict form may ask the jurors to make a finding on each element in each claim and defenses at issue, and will read more or less like a flow chart: "If you found x was true, then go to question 19."

With several claims at issue in a case, the verdict form can appear fairly complicated to the jurors. In such a case, a lawyer may use part of their closing argument to "walk" the jurors through at least what they view as the key parts of the verdict form and how to fill it out.

Trial Briefs

A trial judge may have hundreds of cases to manage at any point in time. And many of the pretrial activities may have been farmed out to a magistrate or discovery master to deal with in the first instance, and then just reviewed and approved by the trial judge. So the trial judge may not be that familiar with any particular case until relatively late in the process.

Further, the law in the U.S. is highly developed, with decades of case law surrounding, interpreting, and influencing the application of each point of law. Many trial judges were former prosecutors or defenders. They may not have a great deal of fluency in civil claims to begin with.

These dynamics work to the detriment of both parties, who rely on the trial judge to make thoughtful decisions almost immediately on a host of really critical issues. The judge must decide questions about which evidence is or isn't coming into the trial; about which witnesses can and cannot testify; what jury instructions should be included and excluded, etc.

To get the trial court up to speed quickly, each party will submit a "trial brief." The trial brief can be thought of as a detailed summary of the case. It will likely include:

- An introduction or preliminary statement that introduces the parties and explains the claims at issue and each party's contentions.

- A procedural history of the case so the court can be fresh on what motions were filed, what the positions were of the parties on key issues, and how they were resolved.

- A statement of the facts in the form of a narrative that introduces the judge to the evidence that will be presented.

- A "question presented," followed by a short summary of the argument. It puts the facts together with the legal issues to explain the party's basic theory of how the case comes together based on the relevant evidence.

- Identification of some of the key evidentiary issues that are going to come up, placing them into the proper context.

All of this should ideally be very succinct and readable. If it is extremely detailed, then it becomes less useful. Instead, it should flag the key points so the judge knows what to look for in the blur of the evidence coming.

> The facts presented in a **trial brief** must be stated fairly and accurately, and "bad" facts are often fronted and put into the proper context so that they are not a surprise.
>
> The statement of facts should not include legal argument or conclusions but should be written in a way sympathetic to the ultimate position of the party submitting it.

Opening Statements

Each party must prepare its opening statement to the jury. The opening statement is one of the rare opportunities during the trial that the trial lawyers have to speak directly to the jury.

The opening statement differs from the closing statement in that it is impermissible to include argument. It is a persuasive—primarily factual—recitation that helps the jurors understand the case, familiarizes them with the key evidence they are going to see, and puts the facts into some context for them.

During the trial, the evidence will develop in the order in which the witnesses are presented, and not necessarily in the order most conducive to the jurors taking in and understanding the significance of the facts. Because the opening argument is a cohesive speech, it is an important opportunity to tell the party's story and the evidence that will be presented to support that story in a more logical order.

Like the trial brief, the opening statement cannot ignore unhelpful facts. Instead, it must incorporate those facts into the story to explain why they are irrelevant, misleading, and/or insignificant.

The party's overall theme should be apparent from listening to the opening statement. As the jurors listen to the evidence, they will hopefully remember the themes the parties set up in their opening statements. Hopefully, their own thoughts about the facts will coalesce around a theme that explains what happened in the case.

The opening statement is also a dramatic moment in the case and should capture the jurors' attention. Pulling people out of their daily lives and obligations is a little less painful if they understand that important issues are at stake in the case, and if the presentations are as entertaining as possible.

Finally, the opening statement is another opportunity for the lawyer to build rapport with the jurors. Ideally, the jurors will come away from it with a neutral or positive impression of the lawyer, making them at least receptive to hearing a lot more from the lawyer and their team.

A typical opening statement:

- Starts with a relatively dramatic and very brief overview of the truly key facts and what the case is about

- Introduces the lawyer's client and the other players in the case

- Introduces the key witnesses and what they are likely to address in their testimony

- Displays key exhibits, as long as the lawyer and judge are comfortable that they will ultimately come into evidence

- Includes demonstrative exhibits clarifying the issues in the case

- May include a preview of the legal principles in the case, but will not argue for applying the facts to that law, which is impermissible

- Ends by asking the jurors to reach a particular verdict after they have heard the evidence.

Closing Argument Outline

As usual, operating on the principle that it makes it easier to get to your destination if you know where it is early on, trial lawyers will prepare at least an outline for their eventual closing argument.

The closing argument is the final presentation. It reminds the jurors of the key facts and shows them the key documents and quotations from the witnesses' testimony. It then ties all this together with the jury instructions to explain how the party's interpretation of the facts should lead the jury to the desired verdict.

The closing argument is the lawyer's big chance to pull their case together in the minds of the jurors. Jurors are not supposed to consider the closing argument in their deliberations because it is not evidence. But they will appreciate being reminded of the key facts and the inferences that can be drawn from everything they have seen at the trial pulled together for them.

Hopefully, the lawyer has earned credibility along the way and the jurors have seen them deliver on the facts promised in the opening argument throughout the trial. If so, the jurors may argue in support of the lawyer's theory of the case when they are in the deliberation room.

A typical closing argument:

- Reiterates and displays the key facts

- Draws reasonable inferences from the evidence

- Identifies and argues about material gaps in the opponent's presentation

- Highlights weaknesses and inconsistencies in the opponent's case

- Suggests a motive for or otherwise explains those weakness and inconsistencies

- Includes a presentation of the key jury instructions

- Walks through portions of the verdict form and how it should be filled out.

Although the lawyer should prepare at least some outline in advance, it should be viewed as a work in progress, as it is helpful to include actual quotations from the case in the closing. These quotations should be included in the witnesses' examination outlines.

The closing argument is a great time to present visual evidence—preparing slides of the key documents and testimony that can help pull together the story. Very often the trial team and the graphics people will have spent at least a few sleepless nights during the trial preparing the various parts of the closing argument.

Trial Notebooks

There is no magic to the trial notebook. This is a binder that is prepared for the lawyer so as to have all the key items ready at a moment's notice.

It will include much of the work product described above, including:

- the motions *in limine* and pocket briefs

- the neutral statement of the case

- the trial briefs

- the witness and exhibit lists

- the voir dire questions

- the opening statement or the outline of it

- the jury instructions.

It may also include the outline for the closing argument.

Mock Trials

Before the real trial starts, each party may hold one or more "mock trials" to hone their trial presentation. There are different styles and methods, but the basic idea is to hold an abbreviated and inexpensive version of the trial. The presentations should sufficiently simulate the key facts and themes of the trial so the party can get a read on what a real jury would think of it.

Mock trials can be critical to getting an honest read on one's own case. It is valuable for trial lawyers steeped in the case for months or years to hear the first impressions of people taking the information in for the very first time. For example, the team may learn an important point was not noticed or that the jurors got hung up on something insignificant.

This is a process that the lawyers and/or jury consultant may assist with or may run for the client.

It is important that the mock jury is a representative sample from the actual jury pool where the case is to be tried. Some companies will assemble these jurors from around the community, or the law firm may hire jurors from a temp agency. Like a real trial, the lawyers may do some version of voir dire with the jurors ahead of time. This may help them gauge what types of backgrounds and experiences may affect attitudes toward their case.

It is also very critical to present a solid presentation on behalf of the opponent. The exercise is less useful if the opponent's presentation at the mock trial is not as effective as it will likely be at the actual trial.

Because the trial team has been steeped in their side of the case for months, or maybe even years, it's helpful to have someone not on the trial team zealously present the opponent's case.

The actual mock trial can be as extensive or as abbreviated as the client wants. If very abbreviated, then the client might conduct a few mock trials. This permits the party to highlight different themes in them or simulate various trial scenarios where certain evidence has been excluded or presented in a different way. This provides valuable feedback on how the lawyers might tweak the trial presentation for maximum impact, or how the dynamics of the case might change if a motion *in limine* were granted or denied.

Perhaps the shortest version of mock trial is a simple "clopening." This rolls the entire trial presentation, both facts and law, into a single opening-closing argument for each party.

Alternatively, a party might hold a more traditional mock trial presentation where the lawyers practice their opening argument, present key witnesses and facts, and then give a closing statement. But this would all take place during a day or half day, rather than a week.

Another variety of mock trial is where each mock juror's feedback is captured on a real time basis through a handheld device. By capturing this data, the trial team can see which arguments and facts resonated positively with the mock jurors and which did not, in real time.

Mock trial is an extremely useful tool. By polling the mock jurors, the lawyers can get real, sometimes shocking insights into their case. For lawyers that have been living and breathing the case for months, it is helpful to learn even which facts didn't really come across to the jurors, and where they need to devote more emphasis. They can also discover which parts were confusing and why, and smooth those parts out. On many occasions at my firm, the insights gathered during the mock turned a losing case into a winner.

CHAPTER TEN

TRIAL BASICS

Even for many litigators, a trial is unfamiliar territory. There is even a saying that cases settle "on the courthouse steps." This is because many litigants, as well as their litigation counsel, do not want to take on the risk of trial.

While every trial has a certain amount of risk, trial practice is a skill like anything else, and it can be done in a way that minimizes the risk and uncertainty. My firm has had a win rate of almost 90 percent for the last two decades, so I know this is true.

It is absolutely critical to read about what happens at trial, as it explains the endgame. If the reader can visualize and understand what will happen at trial, they will have a much better understanding of all the steps leading to the trial and how to best tackle them. They will know where to focus their efforts and will conserve resources and get better results along the way.

Indeed, that is one of the major themes of this book: know where you're going at all times.

Witnesses

At trial, after the opening statement, the plaintiff's lawyer will begin presenting their witnesses.

The order of witnesses will be carefully chosen to convey the plaintiff's story so the evidence is understandable to the jurors. The friendly witnesses will appear through direct examination and be cross-examined by the defendant.

Some of the plaintiff's evidence may need to be presented through adverse witnesses. For example, at least some of the proof of how the accused product works in a patent case will need to come from adverse witnesses. Those witnesses will, therefore, be cross-examined in the plaintiff's case.

After the plaintiff is done with its case, the defendant will put on its case.

For each witness, the lawyers are meeting specific objectives through that witness' testimony, including eliciting the information and introducing the exhibits available through that witness.

A witness' job is to enable the lawyer to present the evidence they have that establishes part or all of one or more claims or defenses. Part of this requires answering questions sufficient to lay the foundation for the knowledge of the evidence they are presenting.

Witnesses should be on the stand long enough to do what they need to do and no longer. Cross-examination of the witness is limited to subjects raised in direct examination. Straying outside of what is necessary during direct examination may create additional avenues for attack during cross-examination.

Along the way in trial, the lawyers will be listening to the evidence presented and matching it with what they need to prove. They may discover that certain necessary evidence they anticipated from one witness has been presented sufficiently by another witness. In such a case, they may consider not presenting the witness they planned to present, or they may present more limited testimony from that witness.

This is helpful because trial time is usually very limited. This saves time for the points that do still need to be established.

It is also helpful because the longer the witness is up on the stand, generally the more risk there is to the party presenting that witness. Witnesses can get tired or lose concentration and get sloppy and provide a helpful sound bite for opposing counsel. Getting them on and off the stand "safely" is the goal.

Witness preparation is required for all witnesses, and judges can get ugly if they believe a witness has not been prepared. Like a deposition, trial testimony is not a casual process, and witnesses should prepare so the examination process is efficient and helpful to the jury.

Witness prep must be done for each witness appearing at trial, whether or not they were previously prepared for deposition. Witness prep for trial is more extensive, as it includes preparation of direct testimony which is not required for deposition. It is also important to work with the witness to ensure that they use language readily understandable to the jurors and can provide explanations where necessary.

> Sometimes the opponent has a misleading theme.
>
> An unwary witness can fall into the trap of saying something that seems innocuous but can be misused by the opponent.
>
> **Witness prep** helps the witness recognize that kind of situation.
>
> Witness prep also helps the witness consider how a sloppy answer could advance the opponent's narrative and instead present a more detailed or fulsome response that cannot be taken out of context.

A proper witness preparation includes discussing all the issues that may arise in their testimony on cross-examination as well. At this point, which might be several months after their deposition, the opponent may have developed rebuttal arguments that were not brought out at deposition and which should be discussed.

Additionally, the witness should review the documents to be referenced in their examination. They should get used to answering the questions needed to lay the foundation for the admissibility of those exhibits, which was not necessary at deposition.

A witness should reread their deposition testimony and any sworn statements they have made along the way, such as in affidavits, declarations, or even in pleadings, if they are a company witness.

More broadly, the witness should understand the themes of the case on both sides and where their testimony fits.

This witness prep also involves practice: asking the questions on direct and cross, and listening to and discussing the responses the witness gives. Some answers will come out awkward, unnecessarily complicated, confused, etc., so this discussion can help smooth out those bumps.

Like a deposition, trial testimony is a formal interrogation that requires active listening by the witness and the lawyer. Practicing these techniques can make the presentation smoother and reduce the anxiety of the witness.

For key witnesses, a "black-hat" mock cross-examination by a relatively aggressive questioner can help prepare the witness for the actual cross-examination when it comes up. Ideally, the witness will report later that the prep was more difficult than the trial turned out to be.

Direct Examination

A "friendly" witness refers to someone you want to tell your client's story, or a part of it. That presentation should unfold as a story, with the attention staying on the witness as opposed to the lawyer asking the questions.

The presentation should be structured in a logical way, permitting the witness to explain the foundation of their knowledge and explain the facts as they unfolded.

Direct examination must be used to present a "friendly" witness. Direct examination means asking the witness open-ended questions like "can you briefly summarize the nature of your work at the company," "what happened next," "what did you see then," and "why do you fill out the forms that way."

In an ideal **direct examination**, the lawyer's questions fade away and the jurors are riveted on the facts the witness is presenting.

By using this technique, the witness does not appear to be anything other than gently guided by the lawyer who is just helping the witness present the story as they experienced it. This makes the friendly witness appear more credible because the lawyer is playing a relatively minor role.

The "problem" with direct examination is that witnesses can sometimes lose their way a little bit with the open-ended questions. Unlike cross-examination, a witness, particularly if they are somewhat nervous or tired, may answer a "why" question with more detail than is helpful to stay on track and maintain the momentum the lawyer is using to make their point.

This is one reason why witness prep is essential: so the witness is generally familiar with their own presentation and lays out the facts in a way consistent and fluid with the lawyer's plan.

Cross-Examination

A famous quotation, which has now been attributed to more than one person, calls cross-examination "the greatest legal engine ever invented for the discovery of truth." True that.

Cross-examination, in contrast with direct examination, uses leading questions to elicit certain responses from a "hostile"—meaning antagonistic—witness to make a specific point.

Cross-examination is a controlled surgical strike.

Typical cross-examination consists of a series of statements with either a "right?" or a "didn't you?" type of phrase, or sometimes just a questioning tone, at the end of the statement.

Let's say the CEO of Acme Company, on direct examination, has testified that a certain product of their company, on which the opponent's damages calculation will be based, was unprofitable and a complete failure. A cross-examination could proceed as follows:

> So let's explore your testimony earlier today that the PH55 was unprofitable, okay?
>
> You explained that the development costs for the Skiddly Widget in the PH55 were about $1.2 million?
>
> And that on top of that, the per-unit manufacturing and delivery cost for each PH55 was $800?

You explained that Acme has only sold 450 PH55 units to date, correct?

At a selling cost of approximately $2,500 each, correct?

You calculated this by dividing the $1.2 million by 450 units, which is a per unit development cost of about $2,666, right?

And then you added the $800 per unit for manufacturing deliver costs, for a total cost of $3,466.

And so, you concluded, you never made a profit on the PH55, right?

Now [changing tone slightly], the PH55 came out in May 2018, correct?

It succeeded the PH45 version of the product, which was out for eighteen months, right?

And before that, there was the PH40?

The PH40 was the first of these three models, and it came out in June 2015, right?

Isn't it true that the Skiddly Widget was also the mechanism used in the PH40?

And it was used in the PH45 also?

You were here when your production manager testified that 3,697 PH40s and 4,187 PH45s have been sold, yes?

And each of those units were sold for at least $2,000, correct? Maybe even more?

Those sales translate to revenues of almost $16 million, correct?

Subtracting $800 per unit for each unit, see here [up on board] that leaves $9,460,800?

And that nine and a half million is more than enough to offset all of the development costs for the Skiddly Widget, isn't it?

There were, in fact, <u>no</u> development costs for the Skiddly Widget mechanism in the PH55 product, were there?

By eliciting these controlled statements from the witness, the lawyer makes a dramatic point that undercuts the idea that the PH55 was unprofitable. For each question, the questioning lawyer already knows the answer because they have documentation and deposition or trial testimony that establishes these facts as true. If the witness deviates from the expected answer, the lawyer can impeach the witness with this other evidence.

Now consider the following alternative scenario:

So you contend that the Skiddly Widget used in the PH55 is a different version of the Skiddly Widget developed in 2015?

And that there were changes to the Skiddly Widget over time that required additional development costs for the PH55, right?

Ok, let's consider Exhibit 32, which has already been admitted into evidence.

What is this document? [It's Acme Corporation's 2017 quarterly filing to the SEC.]

You have seen this document before, right?

You have been the CEO of the company since 2016, correct?

You were responsible, with the other officers, for making this filing to the SEC, correct?

You take that responsibility very seriously, right?

And you and others at the company scrutinize public filings before submission to make sure they are entirely true, correct?

You recognize there are civil and criminal penalties for lying in submissions to the SEC, right?

Now, please turn to page sixty-six and look at the second-to-last paragraph on that page. It says, "The PH55 product is driven by the same tried-and-true Skiddly Widget mechanism used in the previous PH products," doesn't it?

In fact, there were no material changes to the Skiddly Widget used in the PH55, were there?

Now the CEO has not only admitted that the development costs cannot be fairly attributed to the PH55 product, but also revealed that they are a liar. Which the jury will likely interpret as meaning that anything else they say on the stand, and perhaps even what other company witnesses say, cannot be trusted.

The important thing about cross-examination is to not ask uncontrolled questions. This is why discovery, and in particular depositions, are important: they create the ability for the lawyer to know the facts and therefore the answers to questions they will be asking at trial.

Without documentation or deposition testimony to reveal the truth, the CEO could lie in their testimony with impunity.

Note in the last example there are a few questions to which the cross-examiner may not actually know the answer, but they are comfortable asking them because they will almost certainly get the one needed, and if they don't, then it's still bad for the CEO.

More specifically, the CEO pretty much has to admit that they take the responsibility of making SEC filings seriously and scrutinize them to make sure they're true, and that they know there are serious penalties to be less than truthful in these submissions.

If they refuse to admit these things, then they look like a liar and/or an idiot. Either option works just fine for the cross-examiner.

Note that when the impeachment evidence is the witness' own statements at deposition, rather than the SEC filing, showing the CEO's video deposition testimony up on the screen can be very dramatic and very damning in front of the jury.

Another type of uncontrolled question, but one to be avoided, is an open-ended question of the type used in direct examination, such as the last question below:

> So it's fair to say that the development of the Skiddly Widget was finalized before June 2015, right?
>
> In fact, the Skiddly Widget was developed many years before anyone ever thought of the PH55, wasn't it?
>
> There were, in fact, <u>no</u> development costs actually needed for the PH55 product, were there?
>
> *Why then did you think it was appropriate to attribute the development costs to the PH55 product?*

At this point, the CEO will seize the opportunity to spew a long explanation about why it was really appropriate to attribute the development costs to the PH55, undo everything the lawyer has accomplished, and possibly suggest *the lawyer* is trying to mislead the jury.

Whole cases have been lost because the lawyer, on a roll, slips and asks an open-ended question at the end.

The only open-ended question that can be safely asked of a hostile witness is on immaterial subject matter, and the answer doesn't matter one way or the other. But there is really no purpose in going there unless it helps for some reason with the set-up of the ultimate cross-examination.

Unlike direct examination, which is a story-telling, cross-examination is a surgical strike. The lawyer has specific objectives in approaching cross-examination and prepares the questions needed to meet those objectives. Once they have been achieved, the lawyer is finished.

Evidentiary Objections, Admissibility, and Offers of Proof

Throughout the trial, the opponent may object to questions being asked and to the admission of exhibits.

If the objection is overruled, the question can proceed, or the exhibit will be admitted. If the objection is sustained, the lawyer must live without it or find another way to present the information.

In business cases, many objections are resolved before the trial ever starts. By stipulating to the admission of certain exhibits and resolving "high-priority" objections as to others, the judge and parties can limit the number of objections that must be dealt with during the trial.

For every exhibit or bit of testimony that must be presented by a party, the lawyer must consider possible evidentiary objections to that exhibit or testimony, as well as how they are going to overcome that objection.

They must also prepare to elicit the proper foundation for that exhibit or testimony and be prepared to explain to the court why the exhibit or testimony is relevant and not overly prejudicial.

This permits the lawyer to respond quickly and decisively to objections raised along the way. They may have pocket briefs at the ready as well, for when they anticipate a more complicated objection.

Admissibility: Relevance, Foundation, Reliability

Admissibility involves:

- Relevance: does it matter?

- Foundation: where did it come from?

- Reliability: is the evidence a type we shouldn't trust?

The primary level of inquiry regarding the admission of evidence is relevance, basically whether this evidence has a bearing on the case one way or the other.

- Does it prove or disprove any elements in the case?

- Does it make meeting those elements more likely or less likely?

If so, it is probably relevant. This is usually not too difficult a burden to meet since most of the parties' exhibits are on point for deciding some aspect of the case. However, evidence that is relevant but very prejudicial—meaning, unduly persuasive in a way that is not fair because it will inflame the jury—may be excluded.

The next level of inquiry is the foundation of the evidence. For an exhibit:

- Did the witness receive the email?

- Did the witness note the event in the database for that purpose?

- Is the email or other document authentic, or was it altered?

- Has the witness been to the location in the photograph and can state that the photograph fairly depicts what is in it?

- Does the witness personally know of the facts to which they are attesting?

For a lay witness—as opposed to experts, who may provide opinions under certain conditions—their opinion or speculation lacks foundation, is irrelevant, and will likely be excluded. Lay witnesses must stick to what they personally observed.

The third level of inquiry as to admissibility can be thought of broadly as reliability. Each jurisdiction has a set of specific evidentiary rules that are designed to help the court and parties determine what evidence is inherently trustworthy to admit under the circumstances, and what is not.

One objection that comes up all the time and that goes to the question of reliability is hearsay: an out-of-court statement, made in court, to prove the truth of the matter asserted.

A litigator hearing this objection should have a plan to establish that the evidence is either not hearsay, "non-hearsay," or is subject to one of the many exceptions to the hearsay rule.

An example of **"non-hearsay"** is an admission by a party-opponent.

If the statement is:

- being offered at trial against the party who uttered it;

- is one that party adopted or believed was true;

- was made by someone authorized to speak on the subject; and

- was made by the party's agent on a matter within the scope of that relationship or was made by a co-conspirator as part of a conspiracy, then it is admissible as non-hearsay because people don't tend to lie when they make statements under these circumstances.

Other exceptions to the hearsay rule exist because of similar incidia of trustworthiness being built into them. For example, "excited utterances" are exceptions to the hearsay rule because people tend to be honest when they make such utterances.

Preserving the Record for Appeal

Objections along the way must be preserved for appeal or they are waived. In federal court, at least, if the evidence is excluded due to a ruling on a motion *in limine*, the party must make sure that the court has ruled definitively on the record.

While this sounds simple and straightforward, there can be preliminary or conditional rulings that do not amount to a definitive ruling. The objection may need to be renewed when the evidence is presented or when the condition is met to avoid waiver of the argument on appeal.

Also, if a definitive ruling is later violated by a party, that violation is a separate issue that must be objected to at that point to preserve the issue for appeal.

Further, if the material facts upon which a definitive ruling have changed, the new facts must be raised in the trial court, or they cannot be brought up later on appeal.

The trial court must be given a fair shot to rule on the substance of the objection, and that means providing the trial court with a timely "offer of proof."

An offer of proof may be oral or written, and to be valid, it must:

- include all the grounds of admissibility that apply

- explain what purpose the excluded evidence was supposed to have in the trial

- provide the trial court with knowledge of what the excluded evidence is, attaching it or referencing it specifically if need be to ensure it is in the record.

Objections must be specific, clear, and timely. Issues that are not properly preserved are deemed waived by the appellate court.

The Presentation and Admission of Exhibits and Demonstratives

In the absence of a stipulation, in order to admit an exhibit into the record—meaning, in order to permit it to be sent back with the jury as part of the evidence to be considered in rendering a verdict—the party seeking to admit it needs to lay the proper foundation for it, including eliciting any factual information from the witness needed to establish why, for example, the exhibit falls within an exception to the hearsay rule.

Once admitted, the exhibit may be displayed to the jury, and an operator in the courtroom will put it up on large screens.

To ensure the jurors' attention is focused on the portion of the document the witness is discussing, the operator can zoom in on that portion, circle it, highlight words, etc. It is important to have an operator that can do this fluidly so these manipulations are not distracting for the jurors.

Some exhibits may be blown up in advance and put on an easel. They can be marked up by a witness and be visible the whole time the witness is on the stand and while other items are being shown.

It is critical that the jury can easily see whatever is being presented by the lawyers, or they may have trouble following along with the testimony.

A record must be kept as to which exhibits are admitted and which are not. Typically, the court clerk and a paralegal or lawyer on each side of the case are keeping track of this, but in a large trial, it is not uncommon for there to be uncertainty, so the lists are compared each day and any discrepancies are resolved.

Thoughtful and honest **trial graphics** are critical.

Today's jurors are used to multimedia presentations (TV, internet, cell phone) and, especially in complex cases, jurors welcome slides that clarify the presentation for them.

Demonstratives are graphics created for the trial and shown to the jury to make certain points. Demonstratives can include all kinds of visual and audible evidence, including videos, sound recordings, diagrams, animations, maps, graphs, drawings, models, and simulations.

Whether a demonstrative can be admitted as evidence to the jury depends on its evidentiary character.

If the demonstrative is argumentative at all, it will not be admitted because the jurors should consider only the admissible evidence in rendering a verdict.

- For example, a slide might be used in a closing argument to depict an inference that can be drawn from the evidence. The jurors are permitted to draw inferences themselves, but the party's suggestion as to the inference to be drawn is not evidence. It is argument.

- In a patent case, a slide might depict the patent drawing next to the accused product, with each component of the patent drawing highlighted with a certain color and a corresponding element of the accused product highlighted with the same color to show how the product infringes the patent. This also is the party's characterization as to the evidence presented, suggesting that each element of the patent claim has been found in the accused product. The court would likely exclude this even though the underlying drawing would be admissible.

Arguments can be more subtle than these examples though, including an argumentative heading or the highlighting of certain words.

If the demonstrative is truly evidence and has no argumentative component, then it is a candidate for admission. Such a demonstrative might help the jury to find the piece of disputed evidence it is emphasizing more easily. Having key quotations from the trial in demonstratives, if the judge admits them, can help the jury to remember them when deliberating without having to hunt through volumes of transcripts.

Demonstratives can also be helpful for arbitration, mediation, and other forms of dispute resolution, as well as for settlement discussions.

Closing Argument

After the jury has heard the evidence, the lawyers may make their closing arguments. Unlike the opening statement, inferences and arguments are permitted in the closing, so this is a major highlight of the trial. The closing argument serves many purposes:

- It permits the lawyers to pull together the evidence for the jurors to show how it fits with their theory of the case. This theory was brought up in the opening and foreshadowed by certain questions to the witnesses, and the closing is the time to reiterate and strengthen that theory by plugging in the admitted evidence that supports the theory.

- It reminds the jurors of the key evidence they saw in the case and helps them understand why the lawyer believes that evidence was significant, and sometimes why the opponent's different interpretation of that evidence is flawed.

- It permits the lawyer to address the allegations, suggestions, and implications made along the way by their opponent's lawyers and witnesses, and to point out the contradictory evidence in the record.

- It explains the law being applied and shows how the evidence in the trial meets the requirements of that law to render a verdict for the lawyer's client. Where the opponent has the burden of proving the elements of a claim, the lawyer should be pointing out which elements had no proof.

- It captivates the jury by presenting not only a good story, supported by the evidence, but by appealing to the jurors through the use of the theme that the lawyer set up early on: good vs evil, greed, and the like. Basic, universal themes like these help to explain and bring to life the motivations of the parties as they relate to the facts.

A closing argument is not completely freewheeling. It is limited to facts that were admitted into evidence, common knowledge, and logical inferences based on the evidence.

The lawyer may not mislead the jury, misstate the evidence, or misstate the effect of the judge's rulings.

The lawyer may note, however, legitimate gaps in the evidence, such as things that were not said or documented by the witnesses but which people with common sense would expect to have been said or documented had the opponent's theory of the case been true.

CHAPTER ELEVEN

COSTS AND CASE MANAGEMENT

As you have seen, the litigation process in a business case can be complicated and expensive. It is extraordinarily difficult to budget accurately in large business cases because many events are driven by the decisions of the opponent or of the court, and there are literally scores of variables along the way. Sometimes, a party with resources greater than its opponent may seek to outspend and "bury" the opponent with paper, or go as far as to file multiple suits in multiple jurisdictions.

The following summarizes some effective litigation cost management techniques.

Being Proactive in Engaging Litigation Counsel

Companies sometimes believe they are saving money by trying to handle a problem heading toward litigation without the help of litigation counsel. Usually, this increases the overall cost of the litigation.

First, litigation counsel experienced in the subject can provide context to the dispute. They can often help the client develop possible plans for an early and inexpensive exit from the dispute. Sometimes the lawyer or lawyers can explain the client's or clients' position more effectively and less passionately than the parties can and can bring the parties to resolve their differences without extended litigation. The lawyer can also help the client mitigate damages, and anticipate the opponent's likely arguments and develop the responses to those arguments.

If litigation counsel is hired late, many of those opportunities will be lost.

Second, when experienced counsel is tuned in to the dispute early in the process, they can help create or clean up the fact pattern leading to the litigation so it is advantageous to their client. For example, they can ghostwrite the communications to elicit certain responses in the opponent and/or to make their own client look more reasonable, leading to the breakdown. They can also advise the client on how to properly document the facts and ensure the witnesses are paying attention and keeping records of what is happening so these records may be used later if the dispute winds up in litigation.

Third, informal attempts to resolve the dispute without litigation counsel's involvement could result in the client sharing documents or making admissions from which the client cannot recover. While trying to work things out with the other party, a business executive might share a fact they believe to be true when it is not. Anyone who has prepared a PMK witness knows that one person's view of an event may not be the same as the company's view pulled from many witnesses' recollections and with the benefit of the contemporaneous documentation. Once that "fact" is out there, any correction can be portrayed as a deviation from the truth or an attempt to walk away from the truth.

Thus, there is really no good reason not to touch base with litigation counsel early in the process. If they are high-quality counsel, it will only help. And if you do not trust them to help you solve the problem, then they should not be your litigation counsel.

Analyzing Facts Early On and Creating a Plan

At my firm, we say the first side to recognize what will be important at the trial will win the case.

That tends to be true, but frontloading the factual and legal analysis is also a wonderful cost-saver. Some litigators—forgive me—bumble around the case because they are months away from that analysis and do not have a specific plan in place from the beginning.

As we have discussed in previous chapters, identification of the key legal issues and thorough research into the applicable law to get a fair assessment of the merits of the case should be done early.

If the client has a very strong or very weak legal position, then it likely makes sense to try to negotiate a resolution to the dispute without litigation. If, as is more common, the strength of the party's legal position is unclear and/or dependent on facts not yet developed, then there will probably be a dispute. At least the lawyer knows what they are looking to develop and where there are opportunities to exploit the weaknesses of the opponent.

Thoroughly researching the legal issues early on telegraphs to the opponent that one's client is not afraid to proceed and, in fact, is geared up for a battle. Being able to cite the relevant legal authority and point to the exhibits early on, and explain why the law, applied to these facts, will eventually result in a favorable result for one's client, may be persuasive enough to inspire settlement.

> Too often clients think they should hold off on doing research to see if the dispute will materialize, when that research could eliminate the dispute.
>
> Early investment in assessing the merits of the dispute creates value throughout the lifetime of the case.

Working closely with client representatives while the facts are relatively fresh creates opportunities as well. Getting the lawyer up to speed on the context in which the dispute arose, the terminology used, the key documents, and the impressions of the witnesses, permits the litigator to do two things they could not do otherwise.

The first is to start the clock on their thinking. They should think actively and creatively about the facts in the case, about the motivations of the parties, about the dynamics of the dispute, about how to de-escalate, and/or about how to create pressure to push the opponent to consider de-escalation.

Why have them wait through the early stages of the dispute until the opponent creates work for them? That time can be spent exploring potential cross-claims and affirmative defenses, and/or gathering the documents and other evidence that may prove the merits of the case. They should be working to create the possibility of convincing the opponent that the lawsuit will be a futile waste of money and time for them.

The second benefit that can come from quickly immersing the litigator in the facts is permitting them to get a sense of the merits related to each claim and defense. They can then start determining which of these are more or less deserving of the client's litigation resources to develop.

If their analysis shows that three of the claims are basically resolved or gutted by one admission likely already made by the opponent, perhaps the client can then work on finding the evidence of that admission with little participation from the lawyer, freeing them to concentrate on another aspect of the case.

By having a clear view of the facts as they relate to the claims and defenses, and how they should be prioritized, our trial lawyer can effectively narrow the scope of work early on, which directly affects the legal fees they must charge.

Respecting E-Discovery Realities

Much of the cost in litigation is driven by the discovery process and, specifically, the collection and processing of electronic communications and other documentation.

Keeping one's documentation organized and accessible makes finding and collecting documents much easier. Working with an e-discovery provider, ideally at a time when the company does not have the urgency of dealing with pending litigation, reduces costs. It can help with this organization process and can use state-of-the-art technology for hosting, searching, and other functions to reduce overall cost.

Many discovery vendors can assist companies to design and install document retention and other systems during "peacetime" that will save on costs and attorneys' fees during "wartime."

Narrowing the channels through which certain types of communications flow can be very effective in reducing costs. For example, let's say all communications with customers must flow through a single email address and never through texts, tweets, or other company emails. This will then narrow the lawyer's or vendor's search for those communications from having to include texts, tweets, or other company emails.

For companies with a great deal of litigation, much value can accrue from the planned cross-use of discovery materials across cases. It is expensive to search for, collect, and review a new production every time there is a case, much less to fight over every category that is relevant in a case and whether it must be produced. Instead, considering cross-use enables the client to coordinate and put aside collections of materials that can be produced again with the touch of a button.

There are other ways to limit e-discovery-related costs, which are more properly the subject of books on e-discovery, but suffice it to say that very often clients have not maximized their use of technology and other methods to reduce costs related to discovery.

Being Focused in Discovery

Sometimes discovery strategy is not as focused as it could be, resulting in added costs down the line.

Having alerted and engaged one's litigator early on in a litigation, or before the litigation starts, should result in the preparation of a sensible framework of evidence that can focus discovery efforts. This plan should be consulted regularly by those supervising the case and those conducting the discovery efforts to continue to focus those efforts as the case progresses.

Unnecessary resistance to reasonable discovery is often a driver of increased litigation costs, yet many lawyers seem to regard their job as always resisting no matter what.

Sometimes the litigator and client can identify, up front, categories that are relevant and unprivileged, and with sufficient protections in the form of a protective order, they can avoid much arguing, meeting and conferring, and motion practice by agreeing to produce them.

This can also have the added benefit of breaking down or crushing the opponent's resistance to producing similar documentation because the client has acceded to the opponent's demands and been forthcoming. Meanwhile, the opponent has taken an obviously inconsistent position when the shoe is on the other foot.

Limiting areas of discovery directly is possible in many cases. Besides focusing the litigation resources on the claims and discovery items that are the highest priority, some attention should be given to how what needs to be proved can be proven.

For example, maybe there are several ways to establish facts that are usually the subject of expert testimony. Parties wishing to limit costs may want to consider whether they actually need to hire an expert for those facts, or whether there may be another, less expensive solution.

Usually, discovery is an area where more efficiency can be achieved.

It is important to keep one's eye on the ball.

Depositions are also a big cost driver. They each require significant lawyer time to handle properly, as well as transcription, travel, and other costs when they are done in person. Virtual depositions have become more prevalent as the world reacts to the Covid-19 pandemic. This may cut some of the travel costs but given all the lawyers' preparation and planning time, depositions will still be a rather costly line item.

Again, having a case plan and adjusting it as the case continues may permit a party to limit the number of depositions that must be taken in a case. This is done by recognizing which depositions are actually necessary, and by using other less costly methods of written discovery or stipulations to obtain the same facts.

Talking honestly with one's litigator about reducing the cost associated with depositions should also include discussion of how many lawyers need to attend each deposition and which lawyers should attend.

Often, a litigator can be well organized and handle a deposition quite effectively on their own and without a "second-chair" in the form of an associate who is there throughout the deposition to assist. Very often, the taking attorney will have a laptop in front of them and can email an associate who is working on other things for facts or other information needed as the deposition unfolds.

On the other hand, some depositions are critical, limited in time, technical, or for some other reason, the lawyer deserves help in the form of a second-chair attorney. But choices should be made about which depositions those are.

The partner on the case need not take or defend all the depositions either, in most business cases. Less important witnesses might be handled very effectively by an associate at half the price, plus this provides excellent experience and makes the associate's work on the case going forward that much more engaged and effective.

> Well-trained junior trial lawyers can be a great value for depositions, court appearances, and smaller business matters.

Court appearances and conferences can be analyzed the same way. Is an in-person experience important, or can the hearing or conference be telephonic? Is the argument or conference really significant and requires a partner, or can a more junior lawyer handle it? Are there multiple motions to be heard on the same day, some of which can be argued by a junior lawyer?

If the partner is handling several motions or very important substantive motions, having a junior lawyer there to assist may be necessary to enable more fluid, persuasive rebuttal, for example. But if the partner is only handling one relatively straightforward motion, it may make sense to have them do it alone.

Intra-office conferences, meaning where many lawyers of the same firm are on the call with a client or opposing counsel, add up quickly. Not everyone needs to be on every call.

However, rigid rules about this can be counterproductive if the call involves information that everyone on the team needs. The lawyers permitted on the call will then have to double the time they spend in sharing the information they learned after the call, which might be more expensive had the other attorneys been on the call in the first place.

The main lesson here is to be smart and discerning about how these dollars are spent in each instance.

Composing Teams Sensibly

Many business clients limit the participation of litigators on a case to certain individuals or to a set number of pre-approved individuals. This method allows for greater supervision into what each team member is doing, ensures that everyone understands the role of the team members, and eliminates unnecessary duplication of effort.

However, especially when using a law firm in a high-stakes case, it is essential to permit those supervising the case the freedom to recommend and use varied resources within the law firm and sometimes even outside the law firm.

For example, on a project with a unique issue, it may be more efficient to use a litigator on the team that recently dealt with that issue in another case over a litigator that is on the approved list, for at least part of the work needed to deal with that issue.

Another way to save money is by agreeing to have associates handle a higher proportion of the case. Some business cases are straightforward enough that even a relatively junior associate can create the strategy and run with it with minimal input from the partner.

Not every associate is up to this challenge, however. Care must be taken to work with the litigation partner to select an associate or associates whose skill set and judgment can be relied on to handle a serious business matter.

Clients can save money by working with the litigators to arrive at a solution that provides sensible limitations while retaining flexibility.

A Discerning Approach to Motion Practice

Motions can also burn up a lot of money. There are opportunities to cut costs by:

- Thinking clearly about whether discovery sought is actually relevant

- Meeting and conferring earnestly and actually compromising

- Having a judge that encourages the parties to take reasonable discovery positions.

Motion practice, including research, briefing, and hearings, is one of the more expensive line items in business litigation. Parties can benefit from carefully assessing the various motion options, the likelihood of success, and the implications either way and more broadly within the case, with their litigation team.

Some motions are necessary, but some are not, and there may be other actions that can be taken instead at less cost. Even making a simple rule that a careful analysis and specific approval from the client must precede the preparation of any motion can make a difference.

For many disputes, and particularly for many discovery motions, they may be resolved without resort to motion practice. Judges even discourage motion practice in some cases by requiring not only an earnest meet and confer between counsel, but also requiring lead counsel to meet and confer, or requiring lead counsel to meet and confer in person before a motion can be filed.

This kind of approach can actually increase costs and delay due to the rigid meet-and-confer rules. While it might be thought that this would encourage more reasonable behavior by both parties, it actually creates incentives to be resistant for the party hiding information from discovery.

Further, lead counsel's busy calendar creates a bottleneck for discovery, and lead counsel may not have the patience or time to try to negotiate and resolve all the outstanding issues. As a result, this approach tends to not eliminate disputes and instead simply rewards the intransigent party.

More effective is a judge that enforces the meet-and-confer rules and rewards the reasonable party. A stern word from a judge, along with an expedited and simple discovery procedure like letter briefing, can work miracles. It can go a long way toward not only resolving that dispute but also in encouraging a difficult party to try harder to resolve issues during meet and confer.

Staying Closely Coordinated Throughout the Case

> Active, thoughtful case management between trial lawyer and client pays dividends by keeping activities focused and efficient and by seizing opportunities as they come along.

It is perfectly appropriate to ask litigation counsel for a budget for the case. One problem is that the budgeting is incredibly difficult and inaccurate—although some of that can be dealt with by employing a healthy set of identified assumptions and an ample cost range. The other is that many firms will provide an unrealistic budget to win the business, only for the client to discover later that the case is costing them much more than expected.

A better way to manage costs results from better client/counsel coordination and greater efficiency throughout the case.

This can be achieved by:

- Having a close and honest relationship with litigation counsel

- Asking quality questions

- Providing helpful ideas along the way

- Reviewing the changing landscape with litigation counsel

- Recognizing where costs can be eliminated along the way

- Taking advantage of new opportunities as they unfold

- Reading this book

By having frequent and open communication with counsel throughout the case, in-house counsel can learn what events are coming up and discuss and make decisions about how to handle those events in consultation with counsel.

Part of this ongoing discussion should include periodic updates on expected litigation costs resulting from the various litigation events likely coming up. This permits adjustments of the sorts described above to be made. Events can sometimes be stretched out over time also, which can help with costs.

By comparing the actual cost with the budget, in-house counsel can get a greater understanding of what drives costs and can work with litigation counsel to find ways of reducing them.

Litigation and in-house counsel should discuss avenues for settlement periodically too. They should work actively through the litigation to create a dynamic in the case that postures the client for an advantageous settlement.

Settlements can come about even with a difficult or unreasonable party. But that unreasonable party needs to perceive the substantial risk of an unpleasant result, whether that be a financial risk, reputational risk, disclosure risk, etc. And it needs to believe that risk outweighs the potential upside of proceeding with the litigation. By working closely together and revisiting the settlement discussion periodically, trial counsel and in-house counsel can create opportunities that can assist in creating that perception in the opponent.

Another way to maintain coordination between litigation and in-house counsel is to require any legal research to be approved in advance by in-house counsel. This creates some accountability for the litigators around what research they are doing and how much they are spending on it.

More important, though, it helps the in-house lawyers better understand the challenges presented by whatever the litigation event is that relates to that research, and why the legal research is necessary and helpful.

For example, a motion might present a question about the scope of privacy rights that are being asserted in response to requests for certain information from the opponent. Knowing that research about the legitimate scope of privacy rights will be needed lets in-house counsel understand why that research is needed or lets them pass on enforcing those particular requests.

All this is not to say that in-house counsel must now add the stress of micromanaging the litigation to their plate. This book, and a real relationship with litigation counsel, should allow them to participate at a level optimal for the resolution of the dispute, and helps their litigation counsel provide service at the highest level.

Finally, truly high-quality litigation work in complex business cases, or even in less complex but otherwise challenging cases, is expensive because it is providing a great deal of value.

Quality research and a targeted and dynamic approach by experienced trial lawyers should not be nickled and dimed. Cheaper counsel, or non-trial counsel, can waste a great deal of money by generating indiscriminate paper at every stage, without a clear view at any time of how the case will be resolved, resulting in an endless slog for everyone.

Taking Advantage of Contingency and Hybrid Arrangements and Litigation Funders

In the right case, business litigants can save on fees, or shift fees, by negotiating a contingency arrangement for the litigation. This is where the client pays nothing, or just costs, along the way, and the legal fees are taken out of the recovery.

Obviously, many law firms do not want to take on the risk of contingency work, but with the proper investigation, vetting, and cost control, contingency work can be a win-win for lawyer and client.

> If they have a strong case on the merits, clients have a better shot at obtaining a contingency or hybrid fee engagement, or at attracting the attention of litigation funders for their case.

Hybrid arrangements are another possibility. Hybrid arrangements refer to the structuring of a fee arrangement somewhere in between contingency and hourly.

Options include flat fees, flat fees for certain stages, discounts with success bonuses, discounts with success bonuses that vary by litigation stage, and more. The possibilities for any particular case are limited only by what makes sense for litigator and client and can be molded around the merits of the litigation.

For example, there might be more risk associated with the motion to dismiss stage than with the other stages. In that event, the lawyer might provide a discount up through that stage but a higher bonus associated with successfully opposing the motion to dismiss, and then apply lower discounts and bonuses to subsequent stages.

Litigation funding is also a valuable option for litigants dealing with an important or high-stakes business case who need to hire quality counsel but cannot afford the hourly rates. Litigation funders perform their own assessment of the merits and may loan the party money to fund part or all of the cost of the litigation up front. When and if the party recovers, the funder takes a portion of the recovery.

Parties should be careful about negotiating these deals, as many litigation funding deals take a very large portion of any expected recovery.

CHAPTER TWELVE

EARLY EXIT

As fun as all of this may sound, most parties seek to avoid or exit litigation pretty quickly. Litigation is not only costly and risky, but it is a serious distraction from running the company's main business.

Avoiding or shortcutting litigation is not always possible, if a party cannot or will not simply give in to the other party's demands. If the parties cannot work out an agreement, the only way to resolve remaining issues is to file suit.

However, there are some ways to reduce or eliminate the threat of litigation.

Solid Business Practices

Doing business in an honorable way with one's customers, suppliers, employees, and other business partners can go a long way toward avoiding litigation. Many companies have enjoyed decades free from litigation issues.

> Solid business practices—being a good corporate citizen and treating the company's various constituencies with respect and transparency—can go a long way to avoiding disputes that must be litigated.

Ways to accomplish this include recognizing the organization's tolerance for risk and creating a business environment that permits it to stay within its risk range, using techniques such as:

Setting Appropriate Policies, Sticking to Them, and Documenting Appropriately

The creation of policies and rules that are fair and make sense makes it easier to achieve compliance with those policies and rules. Policies should be subject to regular review, adjustment, and improvement. Appropriate training protocols should be in place. Employees and other constituencies should know and respect those policies.

Making Appropriate Disclosures Where Necessary and in a Way That Makes Them Easy to Understand

Recognizing areas where disputes can arise out of misunderstanding or lack of information, and creating and publishing fair disclosures, can help to eliminate problems or give the company a relatively easy defense.

<u>Being Clear About One's Objectives and Promises and Clearly Communicating Them to Other Parties, Including in Contracts</u>

Much litigation arises from ambiguities and simple misunderstandings between the parties. Clever litigators can usually find a way to argue there is an ambiguity even where there is not.

But they can also recognize that a judge or other decision-maker will see through that argument. It is worth taking the time to make sure the parties' rights and obligations are clearly spelled out from the beginning.

<u>Having Excellent Systems and Processes in Place So the Company Can Meet Its Obligations, Which Includes Reading Contracts and Complying With Them</u>

Meeting obligations requires knowing what those obligations are and doing things consistent with them. It also means the company should not create obligations for itself that are unrealistic or impossible.

<u>Having Protocols in Place to Communicate Effectively When Problems or Disputes Arise</u>

In potential dispute or crisis situations, keeping things orderly is essential. Complications can be avoided by

- reliably capturing the details of the complaint

- investigating responsibly

- permitting complainants to be heard without creating admissions or escalating

- taking reasonable steps to alleviate the difficulty

- following up to ensure the problem is resolved

- properly documenting the encounter

When Disputes Arise, Obtaining Quality Litigation Advice to Understand the Merits of the Dispute and to Craft a Resolution Plan

This cannot be overstated. The earlier the issue is fully understood, the earlier steps can be taken to resolve it.

Sometimes reaching out with the litigator can help solve the problem. Responding using serious trial lawyers with a fierce and well-earned reputation has nipped more than a few disputes in the bud. Sometimes it is better if the parties resolve the issue themselves.

Either way, a good litigation attorney should be creative enough to think of ways the dispute may be quickly resolved between the parties and help prepare communications to achieve that. It is at least worth trying.

Assisting Employees and Other Representatives of the Company to Recognize and Limit Likely Risks

Litigation arguments do not always comport with the average person's view of what would make sense as an argument. As a result, potential risks may not even be recognized, much less dealt with.

For example, companies often use labels on their products like "limited edition." The consumer may perceive that the "limited edition" label means under ten thousand items, when in fact it means under one hundred thousand items, and could say that calling one hundred thousand "limited" is false and misleading. Meanwhile, within the company, this may not be recognized as an argument anyone would make since the regular run of such a product is actually five hundred thousand items.

Helping employees be aware of such possible misapprehensions can allow them to spot and address them before they arise.

Creating Proper Documentation and Document Retention Procedures

Documentation is important to establish what happened later. Employees and witnesses come and go, and their memories fade. Documentation that is both fulsome and reasonably available can help to resolve budding disputes faster. It can also make discovery less time-consuming and expensive if litigation starts.

Regularly Working With Regulatory, Licensing, and Compliance Counsel to Stay on Top of Changes in Those Areas and to Ensure the Company Is Meeting or Exceeding Requirements

Tax regulations, securities regulations, licensing bodies, payroll regulations, international treaties, security and privacy regulations, and state law are all characterized by a complex set of ever-changing rules and regulations that apply to companies and their products. Regulatory and compliance counsel stay up to date on these rules and help companies put in place processes that ensure their compliance.

Working with Litigation Counsel to Ensure Basic Processes Are Set Up to Ensure the Company's Appropriate Preservation of Rights

Clickwrap and other externally facing agreements should be carefully vetted by litigation counsel, including making sure that the company's rights are clear and properly preserved.

Respecting the Intellectual Property, Privacy, and Other Rights of Customers, Suppliers, Vendors, Dealers, Employees, and Other Business Partners and Constituents

A great way to wind up in litigation is to misappropriate another company's trade secrets, for example. Efforts should be made to understand the intellectual property and privacy rights of others, and ensure that employees also understand and respect them.

Ensuring Officer and Employee Incentives Are Aligned With an Honest Way of Doing Business

Certain jobs tend to get the company into trouble more often than others. For example, sales peoples' job is to sell, and that means making the company's products look attractive and offering "deals."

When the salesperson's compensation is based on how many sales they can make, they may be tempted to make the product sound a little more attractive, or to skip certain disclosures, or to offer a deal that the company will not back. Which spells trouble later.

Of course, many salespeople will not be tempted at all, but it is wise to consider where the incentives of employees do not match up with the company's goals and expectations.

Trial Counsel: Getting Disputants to Back Off

As discussed previously, early involvement of litigation counsel permits counsel to head off disputes, mitigate the impact and narrow the scope of others, and posture the case in an advantageous way for the client.

In certain cases, a swift result can be achieved without litigation by convincing the opponent there is nothing to fight about. Sometimes the merits are very strong for one side or the other, or the potential damages are so small that it only makes sense to reach a nominal settlement.

> "Speak softly and carry a big stick" definitely applies to litigation.
>
> Well-prepared trial counsel who has reviewed the facts and analyzed the law can sometimes help an opponent see the error of its ways before litigation breaks out.

For example, there are parties—right or wrong—that bring suits based on patents they know are likely invalid or where they know the infringement would likely yield only a small damages amount for them. This is a good candidate for negotiating a swift settlement.

Sometimes there is simply a misunderstanding. For example, let's say some employees leave a company for a competitor, and then some months later other employees from that company leave for the same competitor.

The company losing the employees might assume those employees are soliciting their fellow employees in violation of a non-solicitation agreement, when in fact those other employees are leaving on their own.

In such a situation, the company hiring these employees might avoid litigation by voluntarily sharing its policies and procedures around recruiting. It might explain and provide support for the fact that the recently departing employees contacted the competitor on their own and that the earlier employees understand their obligations to their former employer and are respecting those obligations.

The key to accomplishing this is the selection of counsel. Because much depends on the credibility of negotiating counsel, it is important to select a litigator with that credibility. It is also preferable to make it a trial lawyer, who will be looking at the evidence to create an understandable and fact-based approach to the opponent. The trial lawyer will also ensure that the process does not involve making statements that might be damaging admissions later on if the settlement effort does not work out.

Litigation Alternatives

Earlier in the book, we touched on arbitration and mediation as two alternative dispute resolution mechanisms. Other options might also be considered at various points throughout the case.

Parties are free to decide how they want to resolve their dispute. They can resolve it by tossing a coin if they want, so long as they agree. Parties have therefore developed a wide spectrum of procedures to cater to the unique dynamics of every business dispute. Most of the alternatives below are subject to alteration as agreed by the parties.

In addition to the creativity these procedures permit, many involve a role for company management to participate. This engenders creativity and may lead the parties to develop a resolution for the dispute that is more business-driven.

Still, most parties involve a litigator for their preparation and are at a disadvantage if they do not.

Arbitration

First, a word about arbitration, which must make the list of any litigation alternatives.

Arbitration is not necessarily a great way to avoid the cost of litigation. The rules the parties stipulate to using may be streamlined. Or they may use some form of the regular litigation rules. If the latter, then using arbitration may not result in substantial savings for either party.

> Some forms of **arbitration** promote privacy but reduce predictability and add cost.
>
> Parties should be careful when agreeing to rules about how arbitration will be conducted when they do not know what disputes they will have.

Further, the fact that the arbitrator is free to make decisions with essentially no oversight does not provide comfort to parties with a serious dispute that needs to be resolved.

Some arbitrators are split-the-baby types who order a compromise solution where the merits strongly favor one side.

This is problematic because the side who got a windfall is now discouraged from being reasonable and compromising when the merits are not in their favor. They know that if they push an issue rather than compromise on it, they may have a chance of winning something they do not really deserve. This has the perverse effect of elongating the process.

The parties often agree to arbitrate any disputes in advance, for example, when they enter into a contract in the first place. When they do this, they often specify the venue, as well as the procedure for selecting an arbitrator or a panel of arbitrators. Because these elements of the process are more or less fixed before a dispute arises, arbitration may or may not turn out to be an optimal resolution procedure for the dispute that emerges.

However, there are business disputes that might benefit from arbitration, such as when the parties seek to avoid publicly airing their dispute, and it should at least be seriously considered as an alternative to litigation.

Mediation

Mediation can really shortcut litigation by getting to the parties' true priorities and figuring out, without respect to the merits of the case, whether they can reach some sort of mutually advantageous compromise.

A mediation does not include the imposition of a result on the parties, as does litigation or arbitration. Instead, it relies on an honest exchange with each party about their goals and their priorities as to those goals. It results in a proposed settlement that incorporates as many of those goals and priorities as possible and compromises on the rest.

Mediation is also a flexible process, with the mediator participating as heavily or as lightly as desired by the parties.

The mediator might help:

- Facilitate communication between the parties

- Elicit information about the true concerns and motivations of each party

- Provide a framework for thinking about the results that might come out of a compromise

- Test the waters on various elements of a compromise

- Work on impressing each party with the flaws and weaknesses in their legal case, so as to encourage compromise

Mediation goes beyond the positions of the parties to understand their true priorities in order to suggest solutions that are in both parties' interest.

Mediation is typically a voluntary process which, if it fails, will send the parties back to litigation. Accordingly, it can be beneficial for the parties to provide the mediator with information on the true merits of the case, including the evidence that supports their claims and defenses. This permits the mediator to use information to tease out the true motivations of the parties and to share their judgments regarding the quality of each side's legal conclusions.

Early Neutral Evaluation (ENE)

Early Neutral Evaluation is just that—an evaluation of the case performed by a neutral early on in the process.

Like a non-binding arbitration, the opinion of the neutral evaluator is not binding on the parties, but it is instructive. Unlike an arbitration, the ENE ideally takes place quite early in a case, before the parties have spent a great deal of money on the dispute. It is much less formal, without applying evidentiary or other procedural rules.

The evaluator in an ENE reviews the merits of the case, including the strengths and weaknesses of the parties' legal positions based on the facts. The evaluator then prepares a reasoned opinion on the likely outcome. This can then help the parties understand how a judge or jury might see their case and inspire them to settle.

The evaluator may also turn into a mediator then and help the parties find a mutually agreeable solution. Early Neutral Evaluations are confidential and inadmissible.

Mini-Trial

The "mini-trial" is a voluntary process, a type of structured settlement negotiation, basically.

The process typically involves two high-level company representatives who make relatively short presentations to each other and to a neutral advisor. The advisor might be a judge. The presentations are along the lines of a summary trial presentation.

After the presentations are completed, the representatives engage in settlement negotiations and might involve the help of the neutral advisor.

Ideally, the company representatives were not previously involved in the litigation and have not personally attempted settlement of the case, so the discussion can more or less start fresh. However, they must have either complete or partial settlement authority over the dispute.

> Parties can pretty much tailor a dispute resolution procedure to meet the unique needs of their case.

Before the mini-trial, the parties come up with their own rules as to the format and how long it will take. The parties also determine whether they will engage in any discovery or other versions of traditional procedures.

Mini-trials can involve an informal exchange of the key documents, perhaps some minimal briefing, and summaries of testimony or short depositions. The parties can also agree to ask questions during the presentations if they want.

The whole process usually takes four days or less.

Rent-A-Judge

Rent-a-judge is a type of arbitration where the parties hire a retired judge to hear the case, but the judge's decision turns into a true court judgment. This procedure usually follows regular court rules or slight modifications to those rules. But it is private, and it takes the dispute off the regular court docket, which can save the parties a great deal of time.

Summary Jury Trial or SJT

The SJT is run much like a pretrial mock trial that one or both parties might use to assess the strength of their trial presentation. The main differences are (1) this procedure involves both sides and is performed under the auspices of the court, and (2) the parties use the outcome as a launchpad for settlement discussions.

A small jury is selected from the regular jury pool and might be told that the verdict they render is advisory. They receive jury instructions, hear opening statements, a summary of the evidence, and brief rebuttals, and the lawyers present closing arguments. Meanwhile, an executive of each party, with settlement authority, must attend the entire proceeding. The whole proceeding lasts one or two days.

After the jury has retired, deliberated, and reached a verdict, the parties engage in settlement discussions. If a settlement is not finalized, nothing about the SJT will be admissible in the resulting full trial of the case.

Offers for Judgment

Rule 68 of the Federal Rules of Civil Procedure permits a defendant in a lawsuit to extend an offer to the plaintiff to pay some amount plus the "costs accrued" to date in the case.

> **Offers for judgment** can create a powerful incentive for a stubborn party to settle.

Unless specified otherwise by statute, "costs" include witness fees, hearing and trial transcripts, court reporter fees, filing fees, process fees, and the like. Under certain statutes, attorneys' fees can sometimes be considered part of the costs.

If the plaintiff accepts the offer, the judgment is then filed, and the amount of the judgment may or may not be made public.

If the plaintiff does not accept the offer within two weeks, it is considered withdrawn, and if the plaintiff's recovery is less than the amount that was previously offered by the defendant, then the defendant can recover its costs from the plaintiff, which again might include attorneys' fees.

Depending on the amount of the offer, the threat of possibly owing the other party costs and attorneys' fees can be a powerful incentive to settle. Some state laws have their own variation of this procedure, with the basic incentives set up in a similar way.

In many business cases, it would be wise to consider making an offer of judgment at one or more times during the case.

CONCLUSION

This book arms the busy in-house counsel or executive considering or facing litigation with a procedural framework that will facilitate every conversation with the company's outside litigators.

Familiarity with litigation procedure and recognition of the opportunities and pitfalls that come with it are critically important when litigating in the U.S. courts. Certainly the merits of a case are very important too. But good cases can be weakened, lost, way too time-consuming, and/or way too expensive because of a party's ineffective use of procedure.

Hiring the right litigator is certainly beneficial to recognizing and seizing procedural opportunities along the way, particularly in complex and high-stakes cases.

Having litigated against many elite firms over the years, I can attest that it is an advantage to have actual trial lawyers as litigators. This is because their focus, from the very beginning of the case, is on what the endgame will be. They will take steps at every stage to bring it about so it is most advantageous to their client.

Trial lawyers will also gather and develop the facts needed to try the case, to win summary judgment, or to inspire the other party to settle advantageously to their client. Many litigators do this, of course, but there is nothing like actually trying cases to clarify what is relevant and probative and ultimately persuasive in a case.

The aim of this book, however, has been to take it another step further by arming the busy in-house counsel or executive considering or facing litigation with a procedural framework that will facilitate every conversation with the company's outside litigators. This book provides them with context and understanding they can use to think creatively about evidence and arguments and third-party discovery that may benefit the effort.

Now, of course, some clients do not want to engage in the litigation at this level of detail and would prefer their litigators to just "handle it."

But others are frustrated or limited by that more superficial discussion. Or they have a serious or bet-the-company matter that could be going better. Or they want to impress their boss with their effective litigation management. In that case, the conversation with the company's litigators—after reading this book—can involve better questions, more sophisticated answers, more brainstorming, more litigation magic, and ultimately better litigation or settlement results.

As a bonus, the closer relationship that can form between litigator and client through that more robust discourse yields benefits in the form of greater trust and better service.

The End

ACKNOWLEDGMENTS

A big thank you to the small village that raised me: my four parents and my aunt, who collectively taught me to read, write, lead, and power through, no matter what the Universe dishes out. This book would never have been written without your love, guidance, creativity, and encouragement.

Thank you to Tony for his love, encouragement and inspiration.

Thank you to my colleagues at the firm. There is truly No Firm Like Ours. And an eternal thank you to Tiffany Garcia, my assistant, who graciously and efficiently tackles any task with a huge smile.

Finally, thank you to all those who directly contributed to the production of this book:

Mike and Pat Cafferata

Jill Thomas

Alannah Link

Katie Chambers of Beacon Point Services

Danielle Decker of Decker's Word Shop

Jen Henderson of Wild Words Formatting

ABOUT THE AUTHOR

After more than twenty years at Quinn Emanuel Urquhart & Sullivan, LLP, the world's largest all-business-litigation firm, partner Diane Cafferata has represented both plaintiffs and defendants in a wide variety of complex commercial litigations. As a Fellow of the Stanford Center on Conflict and Negotiation and with an MBA from the Stanford Graduate School of Business, Diane is known for developing and executing creative strategies that get her clients excellent litigation results even in the most challenging cases.

An important part of Diane's winning approach has been leveraging all of her clients' resources more effectively. Having clients more meaningfully engaged enables the whole team to work at a higher level, getting better results with less stress. Diane wrote this book to make the basics of the U.S. litigation process more accessible to both domestic and foreign businesspeople.

Diane has received several national and regional litigation awards and has worked on many of the biggest and most prestigious litigations over the last ten years. When she isn't advocating for her clients, she enjoys racing cars, cooking, and writing.

CONTACT INFORMATION

I can be reached at Quinn Emanuel Urquhart & Sullivan, LLP, where I reside in our Los Angeles and Chicago offices. https://www.quinnemanuel.com/attorneys/cafferata-diane#.

For media inquiries or to propose speaking engagements, please email: orders@litigationdemystified.com.

LEAVE A REVIEW

Please leave your review of the book on Amazon. In particular, it would be great to know how the information in this book has helped you.

If you have questions, you may send them to questions@litigationdemystified.com and leave them. I cannot promise I will respond to all of them but in any case, it will help me to see potential ambiguities to correct, or a new article or book to write.

Thank you!